ADSENSE²

THE DIGITAL REVOLUTION

BY

KIRK DONOVAN

AdSense^2
The Digital Revolution

Copyright © 2004 (rev. 2016)
by Kirk Donovan Enterprises, Inc.
175 Pratt Drive, Covington, GA 30014
404 317 9662

Interior Design: Flynn Marketing Group, Inc.
Cover Design: Flynn Marketing Group, Inc.

Published by LuLu Publishing 2016
ISBN 978-1-365-39491-1

About the Author

Kirk Donovan is a veteran of over 40 years in advertising. Over 30 of those have been spent in Atlanta as President of Kirk Donovan Enterprises, an Atlanta- based advertising consulting firm.

Kirk started his career in radio broadcasting and sales in Florida and has attained educational qualifications shared by very few advertising veterans nationwide. He completed a Master's Degree and advanced studies at Florida State University in the field of Interpersonal Communication. Kirk Donovan is a researcher, public speaker, and teacher on the behavioral science of advertising. He is also a featured speaker on the National Speaker Tour of the American Advertising Federation.

Kirk Donovan is a champion of the retail advertiser. His knowledge, integrity, and insight into consumer response have made him one of the most sought after marketing and advertising consultants in the United States.

This book is dedicated to all the wonderful people I have met, worked with and taught during my amazing career in advertising. I have learned from them, and I hope they have learned from me. I could not have found a more rewarding and satisfying career. And a special thank you to the love of my life, my partner through this adventure and my inspiration, my wife Claire Humbert Donovan. Without her none of this would have been worthwhile.

AdSense^2

Table of Contents

1. AdSense^2 – The Digital Revolution 11

2. The Leaders of the Revolution 17

3. The Global Village 23
    Most advertising messages are ineffective,
    wasting millions in money each year.

4. My Mother Was a Story Lady 29
    My indoctrination into the world of messages.

5. The Behavioral Science of Advertising 35
    The pursuit of a career. We are bombarded with up to
    5,000 messages every day. The messages become
    redundant, resilient and rhetorical. Why 85% of it is
    not effective, or not as effective as it could be.

6. The Purpose of Advertising 47
    Creating a behavioral response. Advertising
    that entertains, informs or entices.

7. The Macro-advertiser vs. The Micro-advertiser 55
    The importance of understanding the
    differences of the big and small advertisers
    and determining where you fit.

8. Realistic Expectations 61
    Realistically evaluating the effects of your
    advertising dollars.

9. The Rhetoric of Advertising 73
    Why most words used in advertising are no
    longer effective. The best, biggest and
    new-improved just don't work anymore.

Table of Contents (cont.)

10. Positioning...**79**
*The key to understanding your competition
and how to overcome them.*

11. AdSense **87**
*The behavioral science of advertising. Why is
salience the most important, yet overlooked,
principle for the micro-advertiser.*

12. Get Your Head Out of Your Ads......................................**103**
*How egos get in the way of smart advertising
decisions. How local media hurts there
clients chance for success. The "negotiability
nightmare."*

13. The 15% Myth **111**
How economics plays a decisive role in advertising

14. The Statistical Science of Advertising............................**119**
*Analysis of the major media for the micro-
advertiser. How it is bought and sold. How to
analyze it using AdSense, and each media's
strengths and weaknesses*

15. Outbound Marketing **125**
*The story of traditional media and its
importance in today's marketing mix. A look at
major media, the ones that are still around and
the ones that have vanquished.*

16. Inbound Marketing **149**
*The story of digital media, including SEO,
SEM, social media and more.*

17. Paralinguistics..**159**
*The importance of paralanguage, which is not
what you say but how you say it. How to
deliver radio and television copy with credibility.*

Table of Contents (cont.)

18. **Writing Effective Traditional Ad Copy** 171
*How to get around the rhetoric and write
copy that gets to the audience that will
respond today.*

19. **Writing Effective Digital Content** 179
*How to write good content for websites,
Blogs and other digital media.*

20. **The Evolution of Advertising** 187
*The changes in media that will affect
business as we know it.*

Creativity is intelligence having fun!

~Albert Einstein

Chapter One
AdSense^2- The Digital Revolution

Since I first started writing AdSense in 2000 the world has seen incredible changes in advertising and marketing. Not since the beginning of the communication revolution in 2001 has there been such a quick, whirlwind change in such a short period.

In the year 2000, the leading source of revenue for advertising was in newspaper space. But now, traditional media like newspaper, television, radio, billboards and print media from magazines to direct mail have been turned upside down. The industry has diminished. Less than 20 years ago you would have seen a person reading the paper at almost every table at your local breakfast restaurant. Go into one today, and you barely see a single newspaper. Why? Because the world caught on. Today's newspaper had yesterday's news!

Less than 20 years ago Americans the primary source of news came from the 6 pm television news. The major networks, ABC, NBC and CBS, dominated the air. At least you could see what happened during the day of the newscast. That fact alone started dwindling the newspaper audience.

In the late 1980s and into the 1990s the cell phone started taking over the nation by storm. The technology changed just about every day. It seems like just yesterday we could start hearing music, news, instant messages, and look at photos on our cell phone. Just as recently as 30 or 40 years ago our telephone habits, at home and in the office, transpired from the phone handle attached with a long cord, one that we usually had to untangle on a daily basis. Today we go to sleep with the phone charging on the wall socket next to our beds.

The world of advertising and marketing had to change with technology. Yesterday's traditional media had to become a secondary source and a compliment to digital media. Its sole purpose today is to take a back seat and drive the primary source of information, both news,

11

and advertising...digital media. That fact has nearly destroyed major advertising industries and given birth to a whole new monster industry.

Traditional media is now called outbound marketing. Intrusive media sources like television, radio, and billboards that derive their financial life from advertising, have taken a back seat to driving society's buying habits. Intrusive media exposes an audience to advertising when they watch a TV show, or listen to a radio station, or drive by a billboard, without requesting it. We have become used to seeing and hearing commercials by default. It has become a way of life for decades.

The new direction leading to people's buying habits come from choice. It is called inbound marketing. As individuals, we choose to search for a product or service using our cell phones, tablets or computers. So buying products aren't as spontaneous as they used to be. In the "old days," we would watch television late at night and see an ad for a Ginzu knife, pick up the phone and order it. Days later it would show up at our door. Today we go to the internet, search for the category we are looking for and have dozens of choices at our fingertips. We are the masters of our choices. We are no longer the prisoners of mass media choices in products.

Now don't get me wrong. The impact of advertising and marketing is just as powerful today as it was when I first wrote AdSense. It has just changed dramatically. A significant percentage of our population still go home and turn on a TV set sometime during the day or night. And television is the new dominant media, surpassing newspaper. The 24-hour cable news networks were the demise of newspaper and the 6 pm news dominance. But they're still around.

People still drive to and from work listening to the radio, even though satellite radio and personal music devices have eroded its power. They still pass billboards on the road, although the power of environmentalism has diminished their quantity. People still read magazines, but not very often. The direct mail industry has become almost extinct. Today's direct mail comes to your cell phone through social media or internet advertising. And that has led to the near death of the printing industry. Imagine the impact it has had on something as dominant through the years as the US Mail.

In the matter of a decade or two, the ideas in the original AdSense became obsolete. AdSense[2]...The Digital Revolution is now necessary and pertinent. This rewrite will examine new media, the digital revolution, the death of old habits, the changes in the former media powers, and the impact these changes will have on society.

Many of the original principles of AdSense have not changed, nor will they change. Outbound marketing still influences people. Top name brands still need to reinforce their image or they will be taken over by emerging conglomerates. New businesses still have to have an edge over the myriad of competition created by the new media. Traditional media still has its place in influencing our habits and buying power. The behavioral science of advertising has not changed. The Global Village has lived up to its name. We just need a better understanding of its effect on advertising and marketing. Maybe this analysis will last another couple of decades. But watch out-who knows what tomorrow will bring?

14

Computers themselves, and software yet to be developed, will revolutionize the way we learn.

~Steve Jobs

Chapter Two
The Leaders of the Revolution

The seed of the digital revolution began 200 years ago. In London, England, a prominent mathematician, code breaker and engineer named Charles Babbage, opened the door to a future phenomenon. His inventions and work on mechanical calculating machines led to computers. Little did the world know the significance of that important finding.

The evolution of the mass communication juggernaut began many years before giants like print, radio or television originated. The revolution of the digital era ultimately led to putting the traditional multi-billion dollar media into the back seat.

The first American newspaper, the Boston Newsletter, was started by John Campbell in 1704. Babbage's discovery came just a little over 100 years later. But the first commercial radio station, KDKA in Pittsburgh, started in 1920. In 1928 the first commercial television station, the work of Charles Francis Jenkins, began after devising a way to transmit pictures over the airwaves in a process called "Radiovision."

Even though Charles Babbage's discovery came in 1822, the first impact of its power began 114 years later. In 1936 Konrad Zuse introduced the first freely programmable computer. He is known as the father of the modern computer.

In 1947 John Bardeen, Walter Brattain and William Shockley invented the translator, which significantly affected the history of computers. The revolution was in full force. In 1951 John Presper Eckert and John Mauchly introduced the first commercial computer, the UNIVAC computer. And in 1953 IBM entered the history of mass-produced computers with the IBM 701 EDMP Computer.

Jack Kilby and Robert Noyce invented the first "chip". They called it the integrated circuit. In 1964 Douglas Engelbart invented the computer mouse and Windows. See how fast the industry is growing?!

The first internet came in 1969, called the ARPAnet. The floppy disc came around in 1971, and IBM sold the first consumer computers in 1973.

The word processor came in 1979, and IBM started selling the personal computer, called the PC, in 1981. In the big scheme of things that was just yesterday.

During this brief period two young college students from Harvard, Bill Gates, and Paul Allen, created a massive explosion in the revolution. In 1975 they founded Microsoft, which in a short time became the world's largest PC company. In 1985 the first retail version of Microsoft Windows was launched.

In 1975 Steve Jobs and Steve Wozniak began a little company called Apple Computers as an alternative to Microsoft. After a Super Bowl television commercial titled "1984," they introduced the Macintosh to a wildly enthusiastic national audience, creating pandemonium in the industry.

Beginning in 1997 with the "Think Different" advertising campaign Jobs developed a line of products that would have an even bigger impact on the culture...the iMac, iTunes, Apples Stores, the iPod, the iTunes Store, the iPhone, the App Store and iPad.

Notice that traditional media introduced all of these campaigns that eventually would lead to the disintegration of traditional media.

Many of these leaders of the revolution you already know. One of the most impactful generals has a name most people don't know. Martin "Marty" Cooper, an American engineer who was a pioneer and visionary in the wireless communications industry, conceived the very first handheld mobile phone in 1973. It was brought to market in 1983, prompting history to call him the father of the cell phone. He is the first human being in history to make a handheld cellular phone call in public. The first cellular phone sold for around $4,000. Today his invention is affordable to just about every citizen, young and old.

Mobile devices, in just a matter of a few years, became the go-to source for a whole range of digital services that we rely on every day. From booking a ride on Uber to listening to a favorite Pandora music station, or even finding a date on an app, mobile has become a platform Americans rely on every single day.

There have been a lot of revolutions in world history. Most have had an enormous impact on the way people live, and the way the world evolves. But no other revolution has had the impact on the entire planet like the digital revolution has had. In a relatively short period society changed drastically. Whether it is a good change or bad change will be judged by future generations. But for now, the story continues.

Early to bed, early to rise,
work like Hell and advertise.

~Ted Turner

Chapter Three
The Global Village

The global village, as defined by Marshall McLuhan, has evolved into a fierce competition for business. The big devour the small. Mom and Pop had to retire. The survival of the fittest has helped define business success, and even the successful companies have no guarantees of continued success. Many of the mighty fall each year. Even advertising greats like CBS Television once called the "Tiffany Network," suffered a significant downfall in the 1990s. And so did the other major networks. NBC and ABC began the fall around the same time. They gave way to over 100 cable networks like MTV, ESPN, Fox News and Lifetime. It all started with MTV and Ted Turner's worldwide CNN Network, which broadcast the news from around the world, in real time, throughout the day and night.

Is advertising money wasted? If all the business owners who read this book completed a survey, you would see some startling results. Ask those business people if they feel like they've ever wasted money on advertising. I guarantee 99% of them would say yes. Ask them if they've figured out what makes advertising effective. I guarantee most of them would say no.

Remember the old Charlie the Tuna campaign, the lovable spokes-fish for Starkist? Where is he today? In that big casserole in the sky! He had a good job for a long time, but eventually the public no longer found him cute. He did come back for a short period in 2012, and it failed again. Sorry Charlie.

And do you remember the cute Chihuahua that led Taco Bell into the 21st century? He had his 15 minutes of fame but produced no results for the fast food giant.

Why are these loveable characters unemployed now? Campaigns don't stay successful forever. Why? Humans are fickle. The more repetitious a message becomes, the more resilient it becomes.

Increased audience awareness of a product and counter messages from their competition decreases brand loyalty. A business that spent millions of dollars on a Super Bowl ad pulled the ad after just four days because of the negative backlash. The client was Groupon. And remember Life Alert, the annoying message built around elderly people crying "I've fallen, and I can't get up"? You don't see it anymore because it didn't work.

THE BIG PICTURE

According to U.S. Census Bureau statistics and facts from the Small Business Administration (SBA), over 65% of all business in this country will survive their first two years. About one-third of all businesses will fail in these first two critical years. After four years the number of surviving businesses is near 50%. That means a lot of companies that open their doors today will be out of business in a very short period. Every year thousands of people lose everything they've ever worked for in a disappointing collapse. They all had one thing in common when they began. They all had the glow of confidence and total belief that what they were doing had every chance for success. Not a single one anticipated failure.

Corporations and small businesses invest billions of dollars in both traditional and digital media advertising every year. Nearly 85% of that advertising is either not effective at all, or not as effective as it could be. That accounts for a lot of wasted money. Why does 85% fail? This book will focus on some of the reasons. It will give those who have wasted money on advertising an entirely new perspective.

Advertisers and those who make the ads must learn this new perspective to reduce waste. We will explore the "big picture" of marketing and the impact it has on our society.

This book can't guarantee you more success in your future advertising endeavors. But developing a new perspective of the purpose of advertising will give you a definite edge in the battle for the minds of your potential customers.

This book cannot tell you how your business in Sioux City, Iowa can develop an advertising campaign that will fall into the 15% that succeeds. That would take a personal analysis of your business and your marketplace, your competitors, the current economic conditions and much more.

What I will show you in these pages, though, are many of the reasons why 85% of it fails. Hopefully, with that knowledge, you will reduce your chances of falling into that ominous percentage of wasted dollars.

IMPRESSIONS OF ADVERTISING

What do you think of advertising? That's a question I have asked people for over 40 years, and the answers are usually the same. People don't like advertising. They don't feel like it influences them. Advertising is intrusive and unwelcome. Unless of course, it's strongly emotional or amusing, like the old long distance telephone company ads. Remember those? The ones with the sweet little grandmother, in tears, because she got a call from a grandson overseas that she hasn't heard from in months. Very emotional music, very touching message. Reach out and touch. Each generation has their "memorable" ads. In the 1980s and 1990s, it was the little old lady eating the hamburgers and beckoning "Where's the beef?!" Plop plop, fizz fizz, oh what a relief it is! Or those great beer ads, from Budweiser to Miller Light with the classic animated frogs and salamanders doing verbal battle in front of a big neon Budweiser sign.

Other famous campaigns that failed include the New Coke. The iconic American company upset even its most loyal customers in the name of cost-cutting. In 1985 they announced they were discontinuing its beloved Coca-Cola for a new product called "New Coke." The experiment was a disaster from the start and abandoned in a matter of months.

The BP Oil campaign failed miserably after they created a natural disaster in a Gulf of Mexico oil spill. And the Victoria's Secret campaign called The Perfect Body suffered widespread backlash and was halted after a few months. Even the biggest names fail in their multimillion dollar marketing efforts.

How many people do you know to turn on television to watch the ads? Have you heard of any successful radio stations that broadcast 24 hours a day with commercials only? And why did yesterday's newspapers have all those stories around the ads?

We're not consciously aware of each message, but that doesn't mean we don't hear or see them. We are probably cognizant of very few, but the messages are ever-present. But do they influence our decisions?? If so, which ones are most effective? Why do some work and some do not? What does it take to make advertising successful?

The most exciting, the most difficult literary form of all, the most challenging to master, the most pregnant in curious possibilities is an advertisement. Yet, it is far easier to write ten powerful sonnets than one effective advertisement.

I have discovered the most exciting, the most arduous literary form of all, the most difficult to master, the most pregnant in curious possibilities.... I mean the advertisement. It is far easier to write ten effective Sonnets than one effective advertisement that will take in a few thousand of the uncritical buying public.

~Aldous Huxley in "On the Margin"

Chapter Four
My Mother Was a Story Lady

My mother was the story lady. She worked at a radio station in upstate New York and hosted a show for children. I vaguely recall memories of sitting in my bunk bed with my sister, Vicki, listening to my mother tell sweet stories and sing songs.

My father also worked in radio. He was a deep-voiced, smooth-sounding newscaster for the Mutual Broadcasting Network back in the late 1940s.

My first radio job was the host of a radio show on a small FM station on the campus of Claremont Men's College in Claremont, California. It was the summer between my junior and senior years in high school.

My best friend Greg Gatling and I hosted a one hour show every Saturday at six p.m. on K.C.M.C. We were the voices of the four colleges in Claremont, California. 880 on the AM dial and 90.1 on the FM dial. It was called "The Kirk and Greg Comedy Hour," a compilation of our comedy skits and segments of comedy albums from legends of the day like Bob Newhart, Bill Cosby and Jonathan Winters. It was probably the lamest show in broadcasting, two young teens giggling and having fun. And we got paid for it! Twenty-five dollars a week. It was the starting point of a successful career. As you can see, I started at the very bottom!

I enlisted in the U.S. Air Force after high school and served a tour of duty in Vietnam and finished my military career at Eglin Air Force Base. Both of my parents were gone so I was on my own and destined for a career in radio. On the day of my discharge, I boarded a bus and travelled to Mobile, Alabama. It was in the early 1970s.

Those were the days that you were required to have a 3rd class broadcast license from the Federal Communications Commission to be on the air. I studied the F.C.C. manual feverishly on the bus and passed the test.

In early January I walked into W.F.S.H., a tiny 250-watt radio station in Niceville, Florida. It had an audience of about a dozen people, on a good day! Even worse, I started on the overnight shift. Thus began an illustrious career in a continuously changing industry, a career that covered over a decade.

From Niceville, I moved up to the "big leagues," the top 40 AM station in the Gulf Coast community of Fort Walton Beach, Florida. I worked the overnight shift again, but this was a 1000-watt station! It covered the whole city!

After seeing and believing in my abilities, my mentor, Gabby Bruce, program director for WNUE Radio, moved me to the daytime shift. My career continued to blossom.

I worked for a fun radio station in a tourist town. I was having the time of my life. I was developing a "voice" and a "delivery." I was learning a new business. There was only one problem. The money! It was difficult for a young kid to survive back then making just $100 a week. And you couldn't put "fun" in the refrigerator.

Go Where the Money Is

I loved being on the air, but my ambitions went beyond announcing. Very early in my career, I understood that the success of the station depended on advertising revenue. My mother always said that I'd never make any money on the air. "The money is in sales," she said emphatically and repeatedly. So, beginning from those early days on WFSH Radio I would come back to the radio station every afternoon and wait for the salespeople to return with notes for new commercials. These scribbled notes came on the back of restaurant receipts, napkins, business cards, even inside the cover of matchbooks. I spent my time hanging around the salespeople more than my fellow announcers, asking questions, going on sales calls, being a general nuisance. I would volunteer to write the commercials, a chore most of the salespeople hated. I knew nothing about writing ads, but neither did the salespeople. In most cases, they were happy to turn the responsibility over to me.

After two years of announcing, I decided that to make more money; I needed to sell advertising on a commission basis. So one hungry afternoon I ventured into the sales manager's office and proclaimed I was ready to start selling advertising. By that time, I had developed enough of an "announcer voice" that selling ads was easy. I would meet a potential advertiser, try to sell him on the merits of my radio station, and then in front of the prospect write a few cute lines about his business. I would then read his script in my interesting-yet-undeveloped voice. It was a useful advantage. Once they heard their name in an announcer's voice, it usually closed the sale. Most salespeople didn't have that advantage. Most of them didn't have the voice, and most of them couldn't think creatively on their feet.

One of my most memorable commercials was the very first commercial I ever wrote. It was a result of my very first advertising sale. The town of Ft. Walton Beach had one mortuary. The mayor, Maurice McLaughlin owned it. McLaughlin Funeral Homes went back three generations in the county, without any competition.

My very first day in sales I was driving to the station and passed a new business. It hadn't opened yet, and the owner was in the front of the building planting bushes. The sign said "Future Home of Little Chapel Mortuary." I made a quick U-turn and drove into the parking lot.

There were two radio stations in Ft. Walton Beach. The station I worked for was the Top 40 station. The other station was a long standing adult news and information station. When they played music, it was the old standards, like Sinatra and Perry Como.

I told the owner that I wanted to talk to him about advertising on my station. He asked what station and I said, "WNUE." His first objection was that he didn't listen to that station, and none of his friends did either. He said only young kids and teenagers listen to that station, and they weren't his audiences. So I said, "When the people who listen to your favorite station die guess who buries them?!" I told him he needed to brand his company with the future generation that would be using his services for years to come. That was enough to let me continue my sale.

He finally asked what the commercial would say. I said "give me a minute" and walked to my car, pulled out a note pad and pen, and began scribbling a script. Moments later I went back to him and read my copy. "Fort Walton Beach is no longer a one hearse town..." it began. The owner got a big grin on his face, knowing he was going up against the well-known McLaughlin Mortuary. He needed an edge. And he found it. He bought my campaign, and after many months the campaign proved successful. My first sale!

Through the early days of my career, I wrote hundreds of commercials. Some worked very well. The customers got good results and continued to buy the station. I kept my job. But, as you probably noticed, I said "some" of it worked. A lot more of it didn't work. And I didn't understand why. I spent much more time agonizing over the ads that didn't work than languishing in the glory of those that did.

It was very frustrating and perplexing to spend hours creating what I thought was the perfect commercial, only to have it fail. Some even won industry awards. They sounded good, but they just didn't get results for the client.

At other times, I would get back to the radio station with copy that needed to go on the air the same day. In a panic, I would write a quick script, run into the production room and throw it together with minutes to spare. The results? A lot of times they were exceptional.

Why did those spots work while the others failed? What made people respond to some commercials and not to others? The answer created the foundation for my career.

In the last couple of weeks, I have seen the ads for Wonder Bra. Is that really a problem? Men not paying enough attention to women's breasts?!
~Jay Leno

Chapter Five
The Behavioral Science of Advertising

After five years of radio announcing and selling advertising, I moved to Tallahassee, Florida, to attend Florida State University. I worked my way through college as a full-time salesperson and part-time announcer at a local radio station.

Upon completion of my Bachelor's Degree in Speech Communications, I decided to continue my academic career. There were several degree programs from which to choose, including public relations, advertising, even marketing. All seemed to be the logical next steps. But by that point in my career, after years of questioning the effects of advertising, I chose to pursue the study of behavioral science. The degree program was called Interpersonal Communication.

It was a relatively new field of study, the academic marriage of psychology and sociology. I wanted to learn what makes people behave, what makes them respond to certain things and not to others. At that point in my career, I had learned that the purpose of advertising could be defined very simply. The reason a business spends any money on advertising is to get people to respond. It's that simple.

After graduating summa cum laude with a Master's Degree I studied did two more years of graduate study toward a Ph.D. in a specially designed program in Interpersonal Communications. Experientially I was learning the art of advertising. Academically I was becoming a behavioral scientist.

Are you a behavioral scientist? Believe it or not, you are. How old are you? You are a behavioral scientist because you have behaved your entire life, and you have observed behavior your whole life. All I did through academia was learn the "language" of behavioral science. But you have a base understanding of it. Throughout this book, I will tap into that innate understanding, and ask you to use it in analyzing the many aspects of advertising.

This war will not be over by the next commercial break!
        ~US Spokesperson talking to reporters during Gulf War 1

A BUMPY RIDE

Playing the advertising game is somewhat like playing poker. When you play poker, you may win some of the time, but you would also lose some of the time. If you took a course on how to play poker from a leading expert, you'd learn more about the strategy of poker playing, and chances are you would win more. But you certainly wouldn't win every time.

Now, if you knew absolutely nothing about advertising and you decided to do an advertising campaign chances are you would get someone to respond to your messages, depending on what you are trying to get across in the ad. But what do you think are the odds of that ad being successful? Probably pretty slim.

The more you advertise, and the more you learn how to do it, the chances are good that you'll be successful more often, depending on how much money you have to lose trying to learn.

But if you become an expert in advertising, and if you learn what makes people respond to messages, your chances of falling into the 85% of advertising that fails are greatly diminished. Or, better stated, your likelihood of success is much better. But will it work every time? Probably not. It's still poker..

There are so many conditions that could lead to a failed campaign-the weather, the economy, the competition, the location, and the list goes on. All you can do is try to understand some of the reasons why most advertising fails and reduce your chances of failure. But you still have to figure out what will work for you and your business. That takes an understanding of marketing, advertising, and behavioral science.

What I will offer in this book is a behavioral scientist's impressions of why 85% of all advertising is either ineffective or not as effective as it could be. Also, you'll learn the perspective of a veteran of advertising sales, who started on the streets at the smallest of stations and built an incredibly successful career.

With those two perspectives, you could be well on your way to not wasting money. But there are many obstacles ahead. We have little control over external conditions.

A lot of obstacles, though, are caused by internal senses of what we think advertising should do, based mostly on our observations as consumers. So often those feelings blind the reality of what advertising really should do, which is to inflate expectations. Here's a look at the confusing, frustrating, perplexing, ever-changing, dynamic and exciting world of advertising.

Get ready for a bumpy ride.

Advertising is the foot on the accelerator, the hand on the throttle, the spur on the flank that keeps our economy surging forward.
~Robert W. Sarnoff

ADVERTISING IS REDUNDANT, RHETORICAL AND WE ARE RESILIENT

I want to spend some time telling you about the uphill climb that advertising has to overcome in pursuit of success. And it is an enormous rise, with many obstacles. My family told me a story about my late father that took place during his youth. He spent a career in advertising and had the creative mind of an advertising genius. He was always thinking about ways to get messages across. When he was a 17-year-old, living in Oklahoma, he ventured off with a friend to vacation in Mexico..

On the way back, they ran short of money outside Amarillo. It was 1927 and Amarillo was a small desert town on the plains of Texas. In the town that week was a traveling circus. My father, scheming on how to get the finances to return home, came across the circus manager.

37

He offered to parade the circus elephant through the streets of Amarillo with two huge signs strapped over it promoting the Big Tent Event.

For his hot afternoon of walking that pachyderm through town, he earned enough money to get back to Oklahoma. It was his first advertising commission. Times have changed. The messages have changed, and thankfully, so have the messengers.

THE OVER COMMUNICATED SOCIETY

Are you aware of how deeply advertising permeates our daily lives? Think about it. Probably one of the first things you see every single morning is a logo on your tube of toothpaste, and on your deodorant. At least the people getting anywhere near you that day hope so.

Then, a lot of you see the logo on your coffee can or cereal box, and you browse your cell phone to check messages, read some news headlines or check your social media pages. Some of you hear ads on your favorite morning radio station on the way to work. You drive behind a Ford logo on the back of a truck, pass dozens of billboards and signage with other recognizable logos of several businesses, and walk past a guy with a Nike logo on his shoes and an Izod alligator on his shirt. And it's only nine in the morning. Believe it or not, we're bombarded with over 5,000 advertising impressions every single day. When you brush your teeth, that logo on the toothpaste is an advertising idea. And the one on your coffee can, and the logo on the truck in front of you on the way to work, and all the billboards and signage you pass by, and all the radio and TV ads, social media ads and web page ads.

If you're 30 years old, you've been exposed to 55,000,000 messages. That's enough to give you a headache. After a while, it becomes very redundant. We are the over-communicated society!

Also, the words of the ads are mostly rhetorical. How many messages have told you how great the product was, or that it was new, or improved, or bigger, or best or friendliest? And how often have you been disappointed?

We hear about the excellent performance of an on-time airline, but every time we fly it, it gets to our destination late. A bank's advertising focuses on their "friendly" staff, the ones who "treat you special." But how many of the tellers make eye contact and smile at you? Especially at noon on the 15th of the month, when the lines keep getting longer!

The concept of fast food restaurants began midway through the 20th century with two standard messages "fast and friendly". But today, most of them have lost touch with both promises. They hire young kids who, even if they could say, "Thanks for your order and have a nice day," are not trained to say it with a smile on their face. Most of the time, they can't even get the simple order correct. Sounds cynical, but order a hamburger and see if you don't get a chicken sandwich.

And what about restaurants describing themselves as having the "best food in town," only to find when you get there that the soup is cold, the salad is soggy, and the steak is full of fat? It happened to me last night! You've been disappointed more than once, I'm sure. We don't believe the rhetoric we hear or see anymore because we've all been burned before.

RESILIENT REACTION

So what happens when messages become redundant and rhetorical? They become resilient. That means we become strong in our views about deceitful advertising and we don't pay attention to them. They fall right off our attention bridge. That's very disconcerting to the person who just spent good money trying to get your attention. Especially if what they are saying is true!

Remember the uphill climb I mentioned? How do you like it so far? Unfortunately, we're nowhere near the summit. Another obstacle to penetrating the mind of your potential customer is that we don't usually go looking for advertising.

There are some advertising categories that we are conditioned to look for, though. In most communities, we know where to go if we want to see what's playing at the movie theater. We go to our computers to search the internet. If we're looking for a plumber, we go to what used to be the Yellow Pages but is now the internet. And where do we go to compare used car prices or to find grocery coupons? The internet with services like Groupon! For some businesses, knowing where to advertise is a no-brainer. But the chances of the public choosing your link when they go to the internet is reduced without a branded name from traditional media, or what we call outbound marketing. The internet is called inbound marketing. That means they are on a mission to search out your category of business or your particular business. If you want them to choose you, they need to know your name. Some people might have seen or heard your name through traditional media but forgotten it. When they go to the internet, they have thousands of options in your category from which to choose. If they see your name and remember they have heard about you, chances are they will choose you over the other businesses on that page of the internet.

Traditional media has its disadvantages, even though it is still the dominant form of advertising. It cannot be measured easily. How many people do you know to turn on the television to watch the commercials? Who rushes to their car every afternoon to hear their favorite radio ads? Who spends Sunday afternoons driving around looking for billboards?

What about the old major category of traditional media called direct mail? How many people enjoy taking ten items out of their mailbox when only one is a letter from a loved one, and the other nine are ads for carpet cleaning or department store sales? The average life expectancy of a direct mail piece in today's over-communicated society is from the time you get it out of your mailbox to the walking distance of the nearest garbage can. Millions of dollars were spent every year on this medium. But the old direct mail suffered when people could get coupons in the palm of their hands on their cell phones. Another major media bit the dust!

There are well over 50 times more products for each category than our parents had just 50 years ago. There are 50 times more choices in soft drinks. There are 50 times more choices of automobile brands, and soap powders and breakfast cereals. In the car business, there are imports, exports, sport utility vehicles, trucks, small, large, fast, slow, luxurious and clunkers. If Henry Ford only knew what he started!

We do not like to be the recipients of advertising messages. I have conducted countless surveys over the years to determine how many people will admit that advertising influences them. The overwhelming answer is no! It does not influence us! Why? We've all been burned before.

So let's create a scenario. You and I own the best Italian restaurant in town. We hire an incredible chef; the warmest and friendliest employees and we have the best food and a truly unique ambiance. So we put our message into a nice radio ad. "Come to Luigi's Italian Restaurant, the best Italian dining experience in town. You'll love our décor, our warm and friendly staff and our excellent food."

Do the listeners believe it? Probably not. But we are the best in town! Sorry. The message is redundant, rhetorical and resilient.

"Yeah! We've heard that before!

When I was teaching, I always told my students that probably the most difficult form of writing is poetry. I say that because poetry is one of the oldest forms of writing. Most poetry is about emotions, and how many emotions are there? Too many to name.

But in reality, there are only a finite number of emotions. That means that humankind has been writing about virtually the same things for thousands of years.

So what is good poetry? It's writing about something that's been written about before, in a brand new way. You don't want to plagiarize.

When you write good poetry, you must take all you want to say concerning a particular emotion and narrow it down into clear, short, concise sentences in a way that triggers an emotional response. That's not easy to do.

Now let's compare poetry to advertising. There is hardly a product or service that has no competition, so like poetry, most advertising messages must make an idea that already exists seem new or interesting. You have to create a message about something other people have talked about or seen before, but say it in a different way. Again, you don't want to plagiarize.

You have to consider everything you can say to let the public know the good things about your product or service, and then narrow it down into 30 or 60 seconds, or squeeze it into a small internet ad, or a highway billboard that should only use a few words so it will stand out.

And you have to trigger an emotional response if you want any chance of making the message useful. That's where poetry stops. Advertising requires something additional, and something poetry doesn't require. To be successful, it must also trigger a behavioral response. You must get someone to act on your message. Sound challenging? It is. It's one of the primary reasons why 85% of all advertising is not effective.

WHAT DOES WORK?

What about the 15% of advertising that does work? It proves that advertising can be effective. Aside from the bleak picture I have painted about the uphill climb, there are so many indications that advertising is a powerful, motivating and dynamic influence on our society.

Up until the 1800s, only the wealthy afford colognes and perfumes. And what about deodorant? It was 1888. Before the 1800s our natural body odor was natural.

With the advent of mass communication and mass distribution, and with the help of advertising, an entire industry was created. Messages pounded into our heads throughout the years the idea that we have to smell attractive to be attractive. So we are offended when we get near someone who exhibits natural body odor. What was natural through all of history became unnatural in a relatively short period. Communication didn't just create a habit; it created an entire industry, and it changed the olfactory sense, the sense of smell. Advertising is indeed a powerful influence on society.

So how do we figure out how to tap into that power? How do we learn the ways to create advertising campaigns that work? First, we have to identify the purpose of advertising.

Advertising is the greatest art form of the Twentieth Century.

~Marshall McLuhan

Chapter Six
The Purpose of Advertising

Anyone spending money on advertising should ask "What is the aim for this?" That sounds like a simple question, but most people don't have a clue! Most businesses advertise out of fear. "If I don't advertise, how will I compete with those in my industry who do?"

Many businesses advertise because they just think that's what they're supposed to do. And some advertise because they like to. They like to see their creation, or their mug, on the big screen or in print. There is a little Steven Spielberg in all of us.

After years in the advertising business, after countless hours of sales training, sales seminars, and reading just about every book I could ever find on the topic, I realized the purpose of advertising. If you have ever spent one dime on advertising, for yourself or someone else's business, there was just one purpose for the expenditure. That purpose was to get someone to respond.

That's it. It's that simple. All you can hope to do is get someone or a group of people on the other end of the advertisement to respond to your message.

There are any number of ways that the audience could respond. The response could be a telephone call. It could be getting them in their car and driving to your location. The desired response could be as simple as remembering your name, or creating an impression of your business in their mind. It could be as simple as someone muttering "Hmmm."

WHAT RESPONSE DO I WANT?

As I mentioned, there is a myriad of ways a person can respond. It can be an emotional response, a behavioral response, or it could be "stored" in a person's subconscious, where it can eventually be recalled or slowly fade into the mind's abyss of lost impressions.

Under the guidelines of AdSense, there are three things you can do with an advertising message under that umbrella. You can inform. You can entertain. You can entice. Which of these you attempt will determine the potential response.

Some business owners I have dealt with over the years had just one purpose in mind for their advertising. They just wanted the public to remember their name or they wanted to create an image of their product or service. What these business owners wanted is called "institutional" or image advertising.

Ford Motor Company advertises the quality of their product and their people. Their ads inform us of new styles and innovations. Political ads tell us about the positive attributes of a candidate or the negatives about his opponent. Coca-Cola ads have always entertained us with pictures of the world at work and play, refreshing themselves with a cold beverage. Budweiser ads amuse us with animated frogs chanting, "Bud-weis-er."

Sportswear has gotten to be a huge industry, making names like Reebok and Nike household names. When I was growing up, I asked for tennis shoes. Today people want a pair of "Nikes." But do the national Nike ads tell you where to buy your shoes? No, they are just entertaining ads, mostly showing sports stars wearing their shoes or hats or shirts. In many cases, out of a 30-second ad, you don't even know who the message is for until the last 3 or 4 seconds, when they show their logo.

Ads can inform, and they can entertain. The other purpose of advertising is to entice. To entice is to elicit a physical, behavioral response.

The Budweiser or Coca-Cola ads don't say anywhere in the advertisements that you should get one. In most cases, they don't even suggest where to go. It just leaves an impression.

The national Ford ad doesn't say, "Go out and buy this Ford." It doesn't tell you which Ford dealer to go to either. It just sells the quality of the product.

The national ad, with repetitive messages about quality or safety, suggests that the next time you consider a car purchase you will find Ford among your options. It gives you reasons "why," like safety or reliability. It informs but doesn't entice.

But what about the Ford dealer in your city? What should his message be? Should he spend his advertising dollars trying to sell the quality of the Ford product? No. He doesn't have enough money to do that. Ford Motor Company spends millions of dollars annually to do that. His $20,000 a month budget would be less than a drop in the great blue motion of a sunlit sea.

His ads should go after the people who are looking for a car today, and show them which cars he has and at what price. Hopefully, the national Ford ads did what they were supposed to do in convincing the marketplace that the Ford product is worth considering.

The local Ford dealer needs to entice customers into his location. And the people most likely to react have already been favorably predisposed to the Ford product.

Listen to local radio ads for car dealerships. You will be amazed at how many of them spend the entire length of the message trying to sell their image or the image of the brand they sell.

> "It's Sale Day at Fidgety Ford! At Fidgety Ford, we have all the new Fords from the sporty Mustang to the classy Contour, from the rugged F-150 to the family fun of a new Explorer."

Well, you just mentioned the same product the other four Ford dealers in your town carry. What have you said that would make them come to you? "At Fidgety Ford, we have the friendliest sales staff on the planet! You can trust us to give you the lowest prices and best service in town."

Sure! A recent survey I read asked respondents to rank the most respected professions. Guess which ranked at the bottom. I don't know why because I've known a lot of honorable, respectable car salespersons over the years. But our impression of the guy in the plaid jacket with the multi-colored tie, the baggy pants, slick hair and mustache and the big cigar looming from a sarcastic smile, came from somewhere.

The image is enhanced by the fact that it is a negotiable industry. There are so many ways to hide profit, and the car salesperson who excels will give you the illusion that you got a "good deal." In reality, you probably paid the same, or maybe even more, than you would have at any of the competitors.

"So let Fidgety Ford put you in the car you want at the price you can afford. We're the home of the great deals."

Rhetoric, rhetoric, rhetoric! This guy just wasted 30 seconds of airtime and the cost of the commercial.

I always see ads that say "come shop with us and get 0% financing for 60 months." But automobile manufacturers incentives are available to every single buyer, regardless of the dealership they are visiting. So if your ad tells the public, they should drive past two other Ford dealers just to get 0% financing, most of that public understands they can get the same incentive right down the street at their local Ford dealer. All that ad is doing is helping other competitive car dealers sell the same product. What they should be doing is getting you to come to their location.

Remember that you can only do three things with your message: inform, entertain or entice. And you can combine these things. You can get some useful information across in an entertaining fashion. You can entice someone to come to your furniture store by informing them about a sale. But you must have realistic expectations about the results. More about that later.

You can't always expect an entertaining ad to entice someone. How many ads can you describe the story line for, but can't remember the brand name? Probably a great many of them.

It happens every Super Bowl Sunday. Major sponsors introduce new spots every year, and people stand around the water cooler the next morning at work to discuss how funny this one or that one was. But in most cases, they can't remember the name of the product advertised.

Before you can determine what you want to do with your message, we must discuss some of the basic rudiments of advertising. But first, let's distinguish between the big national advertiser and the small local impacts.

We grew up founding our dreams on the infinite promise of American advertising. I still believe that one can learn to play piano by mail and that mud will give you a perfect complexion.

~Zelda Fitzgerald in "Save Me the Waltz"

Chapter Seven
Macro vs. Micro Advertisers

The best way for me to distinguish the national advertiser from the local advertiser is to call national advertisers macro-advertisers. This icon of the industry constitutes about 45% of total advertising revenues. They are the Coca-Colas and Apple Computers, the Reeboks and the Bud Lights.

These are the companies that the average consumer talks about if the discussion turns to advertising. These are the campaigns that garner respect and awards in the industry, thereby opening doors to new macro-advertisers and huge budgets.

For the industry leaders, advertising agencies were born. And to the top of the ranks of these ad agencies went the Harvard graduates or the occasional creative mind in small markets around the country who created hugely successful campaigns. Small markets were their stepping stones. These were the best of the best.

Their gathering place became a stretch of road in Manhattan called Madison Avenue. It seemed natural since the largest numbers of macro-advertisers had headquarters in New York. It sure cut down on travel time!

Madison Avenue became the top of the mountain, the standard by which all advertising agencies were judged. On these streets walked J. Walter Thompson and David Ogilvy, the pioneers of modern advertising.

This is where the macro-advertiser wants to be, and they will spend whatever it takes to be there-- even if it doesn't work. Because if it doesn't, there's more than one big agency on Madison Avenue. Believe me; there are thousands of horror stories about expensive campaigns that garnered less than profitable results.

The macro-advertisers spend hundreds of thousands of dollars producing high-quality ads. They would fly expensive models and an entire crew to a remote island in the Caribbean, stay for a week or more in high priced hotels, all for the purpose of about 30 seconds of footage for a television commercial selling mascara. The client has to pay for all this. How much does mascara cost? ? About $4. Do you know how much mascara they would have to sell just to pay for the location shoot?! Then they have to spend more to finish editing the spot. They've spent $300,000, and they haven't even put one commercial on the air yet. They have to sell 75,000 units of mascara before they even go on the air.

What's even more amazing is that they wouldn't keep doing it if it didn't work. These big agencies do it all the time. And businesses keep putting up the money. It must work,

The macro-advertisers don't buy local news. They buy National news. They buy most of the prime-time spots and spend billions on sports programming throughout the year.

These macro-advertisers hire the high-profile advertising agencies armed with credentials of glory. The agencies procure the finest art directors, the best researchers, the most creative copywriters and fees big enough to pay for it all.

These are the giants. These are the macro-advertisers.

The Micro-Advertisers

What about the businesses that have to advertise to compete in today's over-communicated society and don't have the large budgets available to them like the macro-advertisers do?

I call these the micro-advertisers. The micro-advertiser is the lifeblood of local media and internet advertising. The micro-advertiser supports all the peripheral advertising venues in America: direct mail, neighborhood newspapers, the local specialty magazines, and the cable stations.

These are the businesses that you don't hear people talk about on a day-to-day basis when the discussion turns to advertising.

> "Did you see the new Budweiser ad in the Super Bowl? That was amazing!" "Oh yeah, well you should have seen the new ad for Barney's Ford! It really moved me!"

I don't think so. The micro-advertiser can't afford to spend hundreds of thousands of dollars on the production of spots. They can't hire big talent. There are no travel budgets. They can't afford film production; they can only afford the lower quality videotape production. You know what it looks like. You can usually tell a local commercial from a National commercial just by the quality or lack of quality.

They can't afford to buy prime time ads, and can barely afford radio's drive time.

And they don't need expensive advertising agencies to create their campaigns. They need every dime just to get their message in front of the consumer. They don't need creative awards. They need results. These are the micro-advertisers. They constitute 55% of all the money spent on advertising in America. That's a lot of money! Over a billion dollars a year.

This book is written for the benefit of the micro-advertiser. And for the people who buy the advertising, the people who sell the advertising, the ones who create the advertising and the people who are the recipients of the messages. That would be just about everyone! !

I wrote this book for all the businesses out there that have ever lost money on advertising. That would include most of them. I recently taught a seminar for a group of National business owners. There were about 300 people in the audience. I asked, by a show of hands, how many had ever lost money on advertising. About 300 hands raised. It fits in nicely with my theory that most advertising is either ineffective or not as effective as it could be.

What numeric figure becomes the parameter between the macro-advertiser and the micro-advertiser? It is different in every market.

Based on advertising rates in New York City, and considering the population base there, a micro-advertiser could have a budget of up to $1,000,000 a month.

In any other major market, the maximum budget for a micro-advertiser could be up to $500,000 a month. And in most small markets, they could spend as much as $50,000 a month.

The car business shows a clear distinction. A Toyota dealer moving up to 500 vehicles a month in some major markets could spend $200,000 a month or more on local advertising. But the regional Toyota Dealer Group, which constitutes all the Toyota dealers in a designated area, has a lot more money to spend than the local dealer does. And Toyota Motor Company has, even more, to spend on a National buy.

But that's the car business. There are hundreds of other companies out there in middle America that don't have the kind of profit margin car dealers have, but they still need the business. And they still have competitors, maybe a lot more. They need to advertise. They are easy targets to fall into the category of the 65% of all businesses that will fold within five years.

The macro-advertisers have unlimited financial resources to create their campaigns. The micro-advertisers do not.

The macro-advertisers need help. That's why they have Madison Avenue. The micro-advertisers usually can't afford help or don't think they need help. But in most cases, they do.

People are unhappy (and neurotic) in America today because advertising has caused them to have unrealistic expectations of life, themselves, their jobs and the Fantasyland products and services that are constantly pushed on them.

~Curtis Smale

Chapter Eight
Realistic Expectations

John Wanamaker, founder of the famous old New York Department store bearing his name, and one of the country's first major micro-advertisers, once said "Only half of all advertising works. I only wish I knew which half!" And he said that in 1907!

He knew what he was talking about. He was probably the single largest advertiser in the country at the time. That's even before we became the over-communicated society.

If only half of all advertising worked back then, imagine what the percentage is today. Wanamaker, as a precedent study, reinforces my theory that 85% of all advertising is either ineffective or not as effective as it could be.

It was a lot easier back then. When Wanamaker's ad announced a product was the "best", people believed it. They had no other frame of reference. Society didn't have nearly the amount of competition-per-brand in any category.

Before mass communication created mass competition, people pretty much knew what they needed and where to get it.

Department stores were designed for convenience. More "things" in one place than ever before. As society grew, the need for convenience grew. As technology grew, industries were born. As industries became enormously successful, mass communication chronicled those successes and painted possibilities for a restless America. Mass communication redefined business success.

As America grew, and industry prospered, Darwin's theories became more apparent. Survival of the fittest transcended from the human species to corporate America.

Consumers and the money they controlled were influenced by mass communication to abandon Mom and Pop businesses. Mom and Pop had to retire.

Today's independent business owner grew up watching the rise of corporate America. All that owner wanted was a piece of the pie. And the dichotomy between the macro-advertiser and the micro-advertiser began to take shape.

The macro-advertiser spends millions of dollars creating images, which is critical. How could I sell a Ford Taurus at an incredible price if Ford Motor Company hadn't done its job developing the credibility of the Ford product?

The macro-advertiser can wait to see the results. They know it takes a lot of time and a lot of money to move America.

But the micro-advertisers can't wait. They don't have the money to wait it out. They need it to work now, and they expect it to work now. Individually they can't move America. They only need to move a tiny fraction of it.

Probably the most difficult job I had representing micro-advertisers over the years was helping them determine realistic expectations.

When it came to the micro-advertiser expectations usually exceeded possibilities. And the smaller the advertiser, the greater the expectations. The lower the budget, the higher the expectations and the shorter the shelf life.

They probably know that 65% of all businesses fail, and they won't accept failure. When business is down, they'll try whatever it takes to build it back up. But their patience, like their money, runs thin. So here I come selling them a schedule on my radio station. "It didn't work!" they would say. "Well, it's your first time on the air. It takes a while to build your reputation."

What I'm saying is "you need to spend more money." That's easy for me to say. It's not my money. And it's tough for them to hear because it is their money.

To advertise effectively, you have to develop realistic expectations.

There are two ways to spend your advertising dollars with potential effectiveness. Now keep in mind there are many elements to a successful campaign, like the message and the media selected. But there are still two ways to spend your money efficiently. You can spend a lot of money over a relatively short time span. This type of advertising is used for retail sales events, the introduction of new products, grand openings, etc. Or, you can spend a little money over a relatively long time span. The spending constitutes image advertising or institutional advertising.

But don't expect to spend a small amount of money over a short time span and get the kind of results the other two methods produce. If the other guys could do it that way, it would probably catch on, and they would quit spending vast amounts of money. That is the reality of the beast.

So, how do you determine realistic expectations? Unfortunately, there are no easy answers. Every business is different. I make my living analyzing companies to help identify what those expectations should be, and every business is different.

First, you must determine if you want your advertising to entertain, inform or entice.

Institutional advertising is advertising which tries to create, maintain or reinforce an "image" and using it requires a long-term commitment.

Let's say you're introducing a new soap powder to a marketplace inundated with soap powders. We'll call our product "Kudzu Cleaner."

Now, if you're walking down the soap aisle at the grocery store and you see Tide, Cheer, Clorox and Kudzu, which would you probably not choose? Kudzu, of course. You've never heard of it before. And you have heard about the others your entire life.

There are some Americans who scamper to try anything new, but the percentage is slim. A survey of grocery store managers showed that generic products account for only 4% of sales.

Generic products have no name recognition within the public's mind, just like new, never-before-introduced products.

We have to create an image, over an extended period, chipping away at the buying habits soap-buyers have had for years. Don't think you can do it with words like "new" or "better," because the established products say those things all the time too.

Before Kudzu Cleaner can become a household name, it has to become a recognized name. And that takes time. And a lot of money!

I heard throughout my academic career that the average person needs to hear something seven times before they remember it.

Now we're deluged with messages and products and promises. That Rule of Seven cannot possibly be accurate any longer. With all the clutter you may have to hear something over 14 times before it begins to sink in.

It takes a constant barrage of information over an extended period for a product to become credible. Particularly for the macro-advertiser. The micro-advertiser doesn't have the time. The micro- advertiser's message usually needs to entice an action to occur immediately, or within a short period.

DONOVAN FISHING ANALOGY

Let's go fishing for customers. After all, advertising, in general, is a lot like fishing.

Our job with advertising is to go out and find as many people as we can who will take our "bait." There are essentially five elements to being a good fisherman.

The first element is to know exactly what you're fishing for and where those fish hang out. You need to know the audience you are trying to reach and what their media habits are. I went fishing one time outside New Orleans for redfish. They call it brackish fishing. That is where salt water meets fresh water, or in the bayous of Louisiana. We were in a small fishing boat with a guide who knew how NOT to get lost in the maze. We would ride around for 10 or 15 minutes, and then he would stop the boat and tell us to throw our lines in the water. We would catch 20 or 30 redfish, and then he would tell us to bring out lines in and he would head out to a new location. That guide knew those waters. He knew the habits of the redfish. And he knew when to move on. If we had gone out without a guide, we probably would have caught no fish, and we might still be riding around looking for our way back to the shore!

If you are advertising a children's clothing store that sells higher priced merchandise, you need to reach women with the kids in their early 30s with moderate to higher incomes. Do they watch television? What kinds of shows do they watch? Do they listen to the radio? Which stations? If they are looking online what keywords or phrases would they, likely search? You need to analyze the people who will respond to your message and learn their media habits.

Here is another example. Let's say we're advertising for a Greek restaurant. We need to find as many hungry people as we possibly can. So, let's run a radio ad in afternoon drive when they are driving home and getting hungry for dinner.

If you are a good fisherman, you know the key to success is to go where the most fish are. That's common sense. Radio advertising is excellent for targeting big schools of fish in one place each day. This is especially true of products that reach specifically targeted audiences.

If we're trying to do recruitment advertising for a local business college, we know there's a lot of "fish" searching the internet for "business schools" or "need an education." With the proper message, we know they're hungry for our type of bait.

The next element is the number of lines you have in the water. The fisherman with the most lines in the water potentially will catch the most fish. This becomes an element of how many ads you have the ability, or budget, to buy. With a limited budget, you need to have realistic expectations of the potential results or lack of results.

For instance, if you have a very limited budget you might run just one advertisement on television each day in one place or one program like a newscast. If you put your line in that water for a period, in the same place, eventually the fish in that area, or the people who consistently watch that newscast every day, have seen your message. What you need to do is run your message in the same place for a period, then go to another area in the lake. If you do this consistently, over a long time, you will reach a large number of people. But if you never move that spot the response rate will fall over time because those people have seen your ad. If they haven't acted, they probably won't so move your line to another fishing hole.

If you have a big enough budget to run more than one spot every day, run two or three ads in the same newscast. Over the years I have had media salespeople present proposals for my clients with limited budgets. On the radio, for instance, they would tell me to run a spot in the morning, a spot in midday, a spot in afternoon drive and a spot in the evening. I always told them I was spreading my lines in too many areas. I would rather put all those commercials in one daypart for a period of time until I was sure my message had been heard and repeated to that audience. Then I would move to another daypart and do the same thing. If you do that consistently, over a long period of time, it will eventually seem like you are everywhere. That's how to get the most out of your advertising dollars over time.

The third element in the fishing analogy is understanding that the fish move. They usually don't stay in one spot. If we find a fishing spot that works one morning, it won't work every morning. The fish catch on. When the sun moves, they move to warmer waters. They have the entire Continental Shelf as their stomping ground. They may, however, by being creatures of habit, go back to the same place at certain times. The skill is knowing those times.

The public also moves around in their advertising consumption patterns. If you run the same ad over and over, directed at the same audience, the message becomes redundant and rhetorical, and unfortunately, resilient.

With newspaper advertising, your school of fish on any given day is determined by the circulation of that newspaper. On the radio, it's the number of people listening at any given time. With television, it's the number of individuals viewing any given program on a given station at a particular time.

The next element to potentially catching the most fish is using the proper bait. If you've ever been fishing, you know that there are two parts to consider in determining the bait. You must have a lure. That colorful lure will draw the attention of the fish. Then you need the right bait. You need to know what the fish like to eat. If you're fishing in the Pacific Ocean, with more lines in the water than anyone else, exactly where the fish are, you won't catch any if you are using worms.

Saltwater fish don't eat worms. You need the proper lure and bait to attract the fish you want to catch.

In advertising, the lure is what will grab the audience's attention. No one turns on the television to watch the ads. No one listens to the radio to hear the commercials. No one drives down the road looking for billboards. And if someone is reading something on a web page they aren't looking for the small ads that pop up over to the side. You have to have a message that will grab people's attention. Most advertising is intrusive. You need to do something to make it selective and to get their attention.

I sold radio advertising to a gentleman who insisted that my station didn't reach his audience. After much persistence, he relented. He gave me a small budget one weekend to try it out.

He created the message, a rhetorical, institutional theme with no real reason to shop his store today. On Monday morning, I went back to see him.

"I told you it wouldn't work!" he said. So I told him that if he would try one more time. I would give him a free 60-second spot on Friday afternoon during the peak afternoon-drive hours. "You can say whatever you want for the first 50 seconds," I said, "but in the last 10 seconds of the ad, we would announce that the first 50 people who showed up at his door on Saturday morning would get a free $100 bill." "Are you ready to try it?" I asked.

Well, of course, he wasn't. If I did have listeners, he would have to cough up $5,000. "But it doesn't matter," I said. "If no one is listening to my station, you won't get anyone to respond anyway."

The bait, the message, has to be attractive to the fish, or they won't nibble.

Then you have to put the meat on the line that your fish want. That is the actual message. We will discuss that further in the next chapter about the rhetoric of advertising.

The final element to the Donovan Fishing Analogy is the climate. That includes not only the weather but the economic climate. The good fishing guide knows the fish are going deeper in the water even before we see storm clouds. They sense bad weather before we do.

I work with a personal injury attorney who advertises for people who have been injured in a car accident and need representation. A lot of people settle on taking what the insurance company offers them, but a good personal injury attorney knows how to fight the insurance company to get their clients more money.

Over time we had good days and bad days. I finally realized that more television and internet calls came during rainy periods. Of course. There are more accidents when the roads are wet!

I also represented a car dealer in Atlanta who had an outdoor tent sale on April 1 one year. We spend a lot of money trying to get people to the dealership that day, but only a few people showed up. The reason? There was a rare Southern snowstorm that day! The weather climate has so much to do with the success or failure of an advertising campaign.

But the other climate condition is the economic climate. During a recession, it doesn't matter what you do to advertise your product. Most people just can't afford anything more than the necessities. But that doesn't mean you stop advertising. Research shows that individuals who continue to advertise during a recession, even if they cut back drastically on their spending, come out of the dark period in a much better place than those who don't continue letting people know they are in business. They just have realistic expectations that the expenditure won't get as many results as it did during better economic times. All recessions end. But many businesses don't make it out because they fail to let people know they are still in business.

It's rather disconcerting to think of people like fish. Especially since I'm a person and a consumer who is influenced by advertising. But the analogy can't be much clearer. If we learn to become good fishermen, then our chances of catching more fish increase.

Quality, value, style, service, selection, convenience, economy, savings, performance, experience, hospitality, low rates, friendly service, name brands, easy terms, affordable prices, money back guarantee, free installation.

Free admission, free appraisal, free alterations, free delivery, free estimates, free home trial, free parking.

No cash, no problem. No muss, no fuss, no risk, no obligation, no red tape, no down payment, no entry fee, no hidden charges, no purchase necessary, no one will call you, no payment or interest till September.

Limited time only, act now, order today, send no money, offer good while supplies last, each item sold separately, batteries not included, mileage may vary, all sales final, allow six weeks for delivery, some items not available, some assembly required, some restrictions may apply.

Come on in for a free demonstration and free consultation with our friendly, professional staff. Our experienced and knowledgeable sales representatives will help you make a selection that's just right for you and just right for your budget.

Pick up your free gift- a classic, deluxe, custom designer, luxury, prestigious, high quality, premium, select gourmet pocket pencil sharpener. Yours for the asking. No purchase necessary. It's our way of saying thank you. And if you act right now, we'll include an extra added free complimentary bonus gift, a genuine imitation leather style carrying case with authentic vinyl trim!

~George Carlin monologue

Chapter Nine
The Rhetoric of Advertising

It's enough to make you dizzy, but these are words and phrases you hear every day. You probably heard a lot of them today. You become so immune to them that they fly by you when you hear them. Such is the nature of the rhetoric of advertising.

Our minds and imaginations are plummeted with over 1500 messages each day. That's over 60 messages throughout each waking hour. A message a minute since the day you were born. That's a lot of impressions.

The messages hit us in the form of print ads, radio and television ads, billboards. Every logo you see on a shirt, or shoes, or on the back of an automobile is an impression.

Success for major products and services has come to the ones who could spend the most money and create messages that stick. And even that isn't enough for most because other well-financed competitors outspend and outwit the giants, chipping away at their dominant shares of the marketplace.

The most recognizable names suddenly had to become "new" and "improved." In most cases, it was the same product as before. The only thing that changed was the packaging and the advertising. In our language, there is an abundance of adjectives. In the advertising world, however, we hear strangely few adjectives. So advertisers have abused the privilege of the rhetoric available to them. We're so immersed in "bigger and better" that the effect of the words has become resilient.

These adjectives have been thrown around for dozens of years. It's like the word "love." When someone says "I love you" every hour of every day, it loses some of its impact.

Another analogy is using the word "free." Everyone knows that nothing is free. In most cases, the cost of the item is built somewhere into the price.

Take the word "quality." How many times have you heard that label for a product, only to find out that there are other similar products with better quality for your taste?

Or the word "affordable." To whom is the advertised item affordable? A new Lexus might be affordable to you, but is it affordable to everyone?

Another misused term is "friendly."

"Visit our friendly staff today and see what we can do for you."

I recently went to a restaurant that stated it hired the friendliest people in town. I didn't receive one smile. There was very little eye contact. When my bill was presented, I did not hear, "Thank you for your business." No one taught the employees the importance of nonverbal communication in friendliness. They were taught only verbal expressions of politeness but not how to speak with expressiveness. Very few businesses today share with employees how to use nonverbal communication.

Another example of the rhetoric of advertising is in the word "taste."

"We have the best food in town" or "The best tasting Italian food you've ever eaten."

Doesn't everyone have different determinations of what tastes good to them? What if I told you that I was serving the best liver in town? Do you like liver? How can I be so pretentious to think that everyone likes liver, much less the best liver?!

Haven't you been lured by advertising that says "the best" food in town, only to be revolted by steak that is too thin or cooked too well or vegetables that are soggy? It's happened to all of us, I'm sure.

So what do we believe anymore? Does the rhetoric of advertising still work in our over-communicated society?

How can an automobile ad claim that a new Honda Civic is the perfect car for you? Maybe you don't like Hondas. Perhaps you'd rather drive a Mercedes. All right, then drive a new Mercedes, the perfect car for you. What if you can't afford a Mercedes? It isn't the perfect car for you.

How many times do you hear that a business is "conveniently" located? If you live on the south side of town and hear that a business on the north side of town is convenient to you, do you wonder to whom the message is addressing itself? Convenience is different to each person, yet you hear the word all the time.

With over 5000 messages a day, we're bombarded with the best, the biggest, the tastiest, the friendliest, the new and improved, the most advanced, the least expensive, the most expensive, the most convenient. Do these people think we're that stupid?

Commonly used advertising words become redundant and rhetorical, which eventually makes them resilient. We ignore what we hear because we've all been burned before.

I'm not sure there's a single adjective that has not been overused in the world of advertising rhetoric. Should we take these words out of our advertising vocabulary? It would be impossible.

What we must do is limit our expectations of the results when we rely only on rhetoric. Don't depend on the public responding to these words alone. Misused adjectives that don't work, litter the landscape of failed businesses. The public has caught on. You need to get their attention with the rhetoric, but then give them a reason to see you, or to go to your website.

And like a good neighbor, State Farm is there.

~Barry Manilow

Chapter Ten
Positioning

Before being able to determine which response you want to elicit from your advertising message, there are other behavioral science techniques you should understand. One of the most important techniques is to position your product.

Al Ries and Jack Trout, in their landmark book "Positioning," describe positioning as not what you do with your product, but what you do to the mind of your prospect. The basic approach is to manipulate information that is already in the mind, to "retie the connections that already exist."

The book was published in the early 1980s when the world seemed like it could bear very little more marketing communication. Positioning was a good start on the road to breaking through the clutter. But since then the digital revolution and increased traditional media options have added even more to the clutter.

Positioning, as an advertising theory, introduced a new way of creating and analyzing the message. For the first time, copywriters began using a psychological approach in an attempt to achieve results. The rhetoric of advertising had become so oversaturated that the public started to catch on.

We needed new ways to devise "sneak attacks" on the mind of the wary consumer. With more and more products available to the marketplace we had to find the means to position our product away from, or in some cases, closer to the competition.

What that means is that some businesses realize they don't have enough money to surpass the #1 competitor in their field. But they can certainly cut deep into #3's share of the market. That becomes their ultimate goal.

Just saying "new and improved" or "we're the biggest" didn't work as effectively anymore because no one believed it. The message became rhetorical and resilient.

THE UN-COLA WARS

A perfect example of positioning was the campaign by the #3 selling soft drink brand in the country. Clearly dominating the soft drink industry were the two Cola giants, Pepsi-Cola and Coca-Cola. 7 Up knew that the only chance of getting the kind of market share of Coke or Pepsi was to spend a lot of money.

The other two companies had spent enough money on advertising over the years to solidify their dominance. Even with 7 Up outspending both of them, it would be unlikely 7 Up could catch up Coke or Pepsi. It would take too many years of outspending them. So 7 Up, through a combination of realistic expectations and positioning, created a new campaign.

By determining realistic expectations, 7 Up decided their goal would not be to match Coke or Pepsi in sales, but to climb above the clutter of all the other soft drinks on the market. A much easier goal to reach!

Next came the positioning of their product away from the other competitors and toward Coke and Pepsi. Coca-Cola spent millions of dollars each year advertising two words, Coca and Cola. Pepsi Cola spent millions of dollars a year advertising two words, Pepsi and Cola.

The one common word that benefits from the combined millions is Cola. 7 Up decided to offer an alternative to all those people who did not like Colas, so they smartly became the "Un-Cola." They positioned themselves above the pack and became the #3 selling soft drink brand.

Another famous example of positioning was the campaign launched by the Avis Rental Car Company. Well behind industry leader Hertz in annual revenues, Avis positioned themselves with all the people out there who favor the underdog. "We're #2" they claimed. And "We try harder." The self-fulfilling prophecy led them to become #2.

In advertising, positioning strategy should not be overlooked. If you want to win the customer, you must understand the reasons why they desire your product. You must get on their wavelength. And being the first is not always enough. As Ries and Trout point out, IBM didn't invent the computer. It was Sperry Rand. IBM, however, was the first to position the computer in the mind of the public. Sperry Rand no longer exists.

Part of the reason for the failure of most advertising is the inability to position the product in the consumers' mind. Ries and Trout's book focused on national advertising campaigns that found success through positioning. But can it be done by the small advertiser? If you are creative, yes. It can be done.

For many years, I consulted for one of the country's oldest and most respected Ford dealers, Beaudry Ford in downtown Atlanta. The dealership had been selling Fords in Atlanta since 1916.

Throughout the years, as the suburbs grew, all the car dealers moved out of downtown and into suburbia. Beaudry Ford was the only one left. It became harder to get prospective buyers to drive downtown. We decided to position the dealership in three ways.

First, the fact that they were in Atlanta so long was a positive, because they established themselves with many of Georgia's largest corporations as a supplier of fleets of vehicles. I used that in my endeavors to reach the retail Ford customer. Because Beaudry sold so many vehicles, one positioning strategy was to convince potential buyers that volume selling meant savings to them as individuals.

Trustworthiness and reputation were the focus of the second positioning strategy. How could a car dealer be around since 1916 if they weren't dependable?

The final strategy became their central location. A huge percentage of car buyers still comparison shop. By being in the direct center of the population, it made sense to tell shoppers to use Beaudry as their comparison since it was the next closest dealer to them.

These three positioning strategies kept Beaudry Ford competitive in Atlanta for many years, helping to overcome the tremendous disadvantage of being downtown.

THE WATERBED DILEMMA

Another example of local positioning is specific to a small waterbed store in the suburbs of Atlanta. My client was located near a new shopping mall, at least 10 miles from "waterbed row."

This was in the late 1980s when the industry was peaking. Waterbed stores spent thousands of dollars on radio stations every weekend promoting various sales events. There was a "waterbed war" going on.

On an access road along a major interstate were six stores that continuously participated in the waterbed wars. Each of the stores on waterbed row averaged spending about $20,000 a month on the radio each month. That's $120,000 a month in ads telling people to come to that street if they wanted to buy a waterbed. Different messages, different music, different prices, but all with a common message… waterbeds are for sale on this street.

A few exits away on the interstate was Waterbed Showcase, my client. He was new, and only had $3,000 a month to spend on advertising, certainly a lot less than the established waterbed stores.

The positioning strategy was simple: there is another choice. But how could we stand out amongst all the competitors who were outspending us? I procured a billboard right in the middle of waterbed row. In huge letters it read:

"W A T E R B E D? You're on the wrong street!
Waterbed Showcase, 2 exits north."

The message was very concise, not too wordy, and quite effective.

The combined advertising dollars of all those other waterbed stores were to get people in the market for a waterbed to come to that street. Our message simply offered another choice on another street. The billboard was the most effective advertising that Waterbed Showcase ever did. And it was the least expensive.

These examples of positioning strategy prove an important advertising edict. To be successful in business, you do not necessarily have to outspend the competition. You can win by outthinking them. But you can't hope to be successful in any advertising effort if you don't consider how you want to position your product or service in the mind of the consumer.

You must also determine how you want to position your business realistically amongst your competitors. That, too, is done in the mind of the consumer. If you are number one in your category, you must position yourself to stay there. If you are number four, you must first get to number three then number two. When you are number two, you must continually look back at number three, because they're probably coming after you!

In today's over-communicated society, the battle is for the mind of the consumer. Business is war. Consider some of the most often used advertising terms such as a campaign, a strategy, a sales blitz. This is the rhetoric of war. It can be waged with taste and class. It can happen with daggers. Individual business philosophies determine the type of battle. Whatever tactics and weapons are used the battle is to win the mind of the customer.

Earlier I mentioned the huge number of business failures each year. The companies that succeed are run by generals who understand the necessity to compete and the complexities required for doing so. Positioning is essential in determining the ground rules for competition.

Advertising is, actually, a simple phenomenon in terms of economics. It is merely a substitute for a personal sales force - an extension, if you will, of the merchant who cries aloud his wares.

~Rosser Reeves

Chapter Eleven
AdSense

Stanley Redd is a loyal friend and business partner over the years. He's often been heard to say that I had a "unique ability to point out the obvious." That is AdSense.

Stanley attended a seminar I conducted. A woman described her dilemma. She was running radio ads requesting that people pick up the phone and call her to order her product.

"I'm not getting many phone calls," she said. "I've spent a lot of money on radio. What can I do?"

"Don't buy radio," I responded rapidly and succinctly. "Try television. The phone (this was before cell phones and the digital revolution) is usually within walking distance of the TV. So if someone is interested, they will pick up the phone and call you. If they are driving somewhere in their car and become interested in your product, you are relying on them to remember your phone number once they get to a phone. They would probably have to hear your ad numerous times before they were able to respond. With television, all they have to do is reach for the phone." "I could have thought of that!" she playfully acknowledged. But she didn't. Never overlook the obvious. That is AdSense.

Of course, today everyone has a cell phone in their home, their car, their office...usually in their hand. But the theory still holds true. It just becomes more convenient with a cell phone, and the customer can call immediately. They no longer have to wait till they get home.

Statistical science fuels today's advertising business. Advertising is bought and sold based on statistical science. But, as I described earlier, the ultimate purpose of advertising is to get a response. The future of the "micro-advertiser" will have to utilize the behavioral science of advertising or AdSense.

I want you to participate in an exercise with me. The purpose will be to show you that advertising messages require more than just creativity.

One of the principle ingredients of AdSense is salience. One dictionary describes salience as "strikingly conspicuous." I will redefine salience with an example. I'll create a scene for you so follow along with me.

We're sitting in my office talking. What we are talking about doesn't matter. You can insert your verbal scenario. In my office is a big picture window, overlooking the parking lot of a small restaurant. Again, follow along.

We're both dressed in nice, expensive business clothes, it's pouring down rain outside, and there is no umbrella in the room. I glance out the window and say "Wow! It's pouring down rain out there!"

Now, you heard me. You received an auditory signal. You respond nonverbally by glancing toward the window. And you may verbally respond, "It sure is." Then we continue our previous conversation.

Now I'll show you the impact of salience by adding just one element to our scenario. We're getting ready to walk across that parking lot to the restaurant for lunch. I say," Wow! It's pouring down rain out there!"

By adding that one element the same statement you heard earlier, the one you responded to both verbally and nonverbally, suddenly became salient. It will create or change a physical, behavioral response. In this case, we won't walk out the door yet, or we'll get wet.

Salience, in AdSense terminology, is something that will change, alter or create a behavioral response. In our scene, adding the detail of getting ready to walk across that parking lot to the restaurant for lunch changes a behavioral response. We were getting ready to walk out the door into a rainstorm with no umbrella. Now, we'll wait. We postponed our response.

In all the years I've been involved in the advertising business, through all the advertising "experts" I've encountered, and advertising agencies I heard pitch their plans, no one ever talked about salience. They talked about creative awards and statistical costs-per-point. But not salience. That is unfortunate because it is the most important element of AdSense, and of advertising in general.

To be successful in advertising, you must understand your target audience. Then you must analyze what it is about your product or service that is salient to that audience. A combination of statistical science and behavioral science, not just the traditional statistical way is required.

DEEPER INTO SALIENCE

Here are some other examples of using salience in your thought process based on experiences I've had throughout my career.

There was an automobile dealer called Dodge Country in the northern suburbs of Atlanta. The owner was a long-time client of mine. When I began consulting with him on his advertising, I made some bold suggestions. My advice went against the grain of the traditional car dealer advertising.

Back then the primary advertising medium used by car dealers was the newspaper classifieds. As a society, we were trained that when we want to look for a car we go to the local paper's classified automobile advertising section.

We were also conditioned to go to the theater section to find out what time our movie starts and where to go. We were conditioned to go to the newspaper on certain days to get our grocery coupons. We were conditioned to use the paper to look for job interviews. And we were conditioned to use the newspaper to find deals on cars. Newspaper revenues dominated all other media combined when it came to automobile advertising. Today, with the death of the newspaper industry, all those habits have been diverted to the internet. We use the Internet to see what movies are playing. Newspaper coupons gave way to companies like Groupon. Coupons now are digital.

The reason most of these conditionings were related to newspaper advertising was that newspapers had been selling ads much longer than other traditional media. Television and radio had been advertising forces for less than a century. Benjamin Franklin sold ads in Poor Richard's Almanac in 1733. Newspaper advertising had quite a head start.

My suggestion for Dodge Country was to get out of the newspaper. Try television advertising. Bill looked at me with shock and amazement.

"O.K.," he said. "Justify your suggestion."

There were several reasons for my recommendation. One goes back a long way.

As a young teenager in Southern California, I used to sit and watch television every Saturday morning. It was the mid 1960s, and Ralph Williams had discovered television advertising. Ralph Williams Ford ran 30-second commercials in what seemed like every break. He would pitch primarily used cars, and the spots were done live, so each spot was different.

In one ad he would be standing next to a beat up looking car with a big $999 painted on the windshield. There stood this big, gruff sounding guy in a cheap suit yelling about how great a deal it was. Then he would pick up a big sledgehammer and smash the windshield! "$699!" he would yell! In the next spot, he would have a dog sitting on the hood of another car. He would be talking to the dog about how great a deal this was. I used to laugh like crazy. But I remembered Ralph Williams Ford. And guess where I bought my first car? I always knew that television must be a good medium for selling vehicles.

There was another reason. Just down the street from Dodge Country was the highest volume car dealer in Atlanta, a dealer that spent over three times more on advertising than the next leading car advertiser. This dealership budgeted over $150,000 a month on Atlanta television and continuously sold over 500 vehicles a month. They did it with no newspaper or radio just television.

Now remember positioning? This dealership down the street spent all that money each month telling people who were looking for a car to get off at their exit on the interstate. Every single ad was different. Different sales events, different prices. But every message had one thing in common. If you're looking for a car, get off at this exit.

Well, we couldn't spend even a third of that guy's budget, but we did have one crucial thing in common with that them. We were off their exit.

THE ANALYSIS

Next, I analyzed a statistical consideration. Remember I said AdSense is a blend of statistical and behavioral science. On any given day, anywhere in the United States, only about 1% of the population is in the market for a car. That is your salient audience on any given day. That percentage can vary slightly according to economic conditions, climatic condition, and many other variables. But for the most part, on any given day, only 1% of the driving population is a legitimate prospect. We're talking about a new or used car, truck, van or anything.

Being in the market for a car doesn't necessarily mean you're looking today. Your lease may be expiring in two months. You may be having more and more problems with your current car and feel like it's going to fall apart any day. You may have earned a raise and can soon afford a better car. Your kid may be getting his license, and you're beginning to explore. That is being in the 1% in the market for a car. It doesn't mean that 1% of the population will drive around looking for a car or make a purchase today. So who is the salient audience for a car dealer on any given day? It's that 1% who are in the market for a car today.

As a car dealer trying to find ways of reaching that salient audience, there's another statistic that makes it even more agonizing. What percentage of that car buying population is in the market for their line of cars? Out of all the cars sold in this country, back then the Dodge line of cars and trucks captured about 7%. So on any given day only 7% of 1% were potentially in the market for one of these vehicles. That was Dodge Country's salient audience on any given day.

So why didn't I recommend newspaper advertising for Dodge Country? First, let's look at it from a "statistical" perspective. Newspaper rates were based on circulation. The prices you pay were statistically derived. The newspaper reaches a certain number of people every day through circulation. Based on the number of those subscribers, a price for an ad was established and justified by a low cost-per-thousand.

But as behavioral scientists, we must add to the cost factor a vital element. On any given day only about 1% of the people getting the newspaper would open the classified automobile section! When you buy an ad in that classified section, you were paying for everyone getting the newspaper that day. But only 1% were in a position to read that ad, unless, maybe, it is on the back page. And that was extremely expensive.

Even then, if they were not in the market for a car, they would not respond to your message. If they were not looking for a car the ad wasn't salient. Even if they saw a great price on a car but didn't need it they wouldn't need to respond. No offense. They just don't need a car right now.

There are two things you can do with your advertising message. You can get people to note your message. The more "notations," the better chance the audience has of remembering you once your product becomes salient to them. That means you can reach the 99% who aren't looking for a car today and hopefully remember your name when they start searching for a car, or when they fall into the 1%.

The other thing, of course, is to get them to respond to your message. The ones with the potential to respond are your salient audience or the ones in the market for a car.

I told Bill that if I bought a television ad on the 6 o'clock news, the same premise would hold true for the television as it did for the newspaper. Only 1% of the viewers are in the market for a car. But the rest have an opportunity to note the ad. In the newspaper, they had to turn to that automotive advertising section. And who would spend time in the classified auto section of the newspaper if they aren't looking for a car? No exposure and no notation.

On television, you've got them. And you can show them the actual vehicle in motion, not a line drawing or a hardly-visible picture like you get with newsprint.

Well, I had provided enough information for Dodge Country to try television advertising. But the process of AdSense didn't stop once we determined which media we were going to use. Salience is as relevant to the message as it is to the medium. Here is the thought process used in the case of Dodge Country's creative effort.

Dodge targets Middle America. Middle America is the mainstay of our economy. It is the vast expanse of humanity who live from paycheck to paycheck with a little left over for savings and retirement. Because Middle America accounts for so much of our economy, most advertising is targeted to them.

Our over-communicated society inundates Middle America with a barrage of ways to dispose of what little disposable income is left over at the end of each month. First, let's determine what is important to middle America when it comes to purchasing a car. What is the most salient point?

Over many years of consulting car dealers of all kinds, I've read dozens of customer satisfaction surveys. There were always questions asking for reasons behind their car purchase. There were many reasons. Brand loyalty is important, but not as important as it used to be. There are so many choices now. And so many cars look alike.

Safety is very important, and reputation for dependability, and quality. And of course, style is important. But there's one thing that surpasses all those other reasons in determining Middle America's choice for a new car.

Price? You're close. But let's say we advertised a new car for $23,575. Can Middle America determine what the monthly payment is when you finance $23,575? And can they do it in the time it takes them to see a 30-second television ad? Not many people are ready or able, at that moment, to compute that.

The most important factor for middle Americans in their decision-making process is the monthly payment. How much income do I have to spend on a car payment each month? That is the salient point.

Will you respond to a message that gets your attention, even if you can't afford the product? You may see an ad for a new Jaguar that is gorgeous. It's the car you have always wanted, but if the payment is $800 a month and you can only afford $300 a month, you won't respond.

By using television ads showing several "sale" vehicles with attractive monthly payments Dodge Country became one of the top-selling Dodge dealers in Georgia. Dodge achieved this status without using the traditional newspaper advertising. Dodge spent the same amount for advertising it spent before the television ads. We sold more than 100 cars more a month. We used the same advertising dollars, but we used the money effectively.

By using salience to determine which media we must use to reach our potential audience, and using salience in creating a message that could entice that potential audience to react, we maximized the return on our investment.

This example wasn't meant to attack the effectiveness of newspaper advertising for car dealers. I had dealt with some dealers who were very successful with their print ads. But with continuously rising prices in newspaper advertising costs it was getting more and more difficult to be cost effective. Maybe that's one of the reasons for the fall of the newspaper industry.

Do you see how important it is to consider the behavioral science of advertising? That is AdSense. Here are some other examples of how it works.

I consulted for the owner of an Italian restaurant. That's a tough job in a major city where Italian restaurants are plentiful. I asked him the purpose of his advertising. What was the response he wanted to elicit? He gave the generic answer. "To get more business," he said.

I hear that all the time, and so I want to dissect that phrase, that logic. First, let's consider realistic expectations. Who is the most likely person to come to his restaurant? Someone who is hungry. That's a good start.

Next would be someone who is hungry for Italian food. Then they need to be within driving distance of your restaurant. What can we possibly say to lure this, our salient audience, to your restaurant? "We have great food?"

First of all, no one will believe it. Remember that we're bombarded with well over 3,000 messages each day! And how many times have we been promised things in advertising that weren't delivered? So even if you do have the best food in town, no one will believe it when you tell them.

Secondly, let's say you did find someone who was hungry for Italian food. From where that person is when he sees or hears your message how many Italian restaurants does he have to pass to get to yours? There could be dozens. Would you drive 20 miles, past ten or twelve Italian restaurants, to go to one that you heard about on the radio? One that claims they have the best Italian food in town? Possibly, but not likely. Remember, we've all been burned before.

So my challenge was to find a way to make this restaurant stand out from all the other Italian restaurants. What could I say about this restaurant that no other restaurant could say? Well, in this case, the restaurant did have something different. The building was attached to an old railroad dining car, and it sat right next to an old-but-still-used railroad track. I built my campaign around that as the salient point.

"Imagine," the copy said, "sitting in a little trattoria on a hillside near Rome. The music of Italy fills the room." Cue the music. "A train streaks past your window." Cue sound effect of a train. "You're enjoying the flavors of classic Italy and well, you don't have far to go."

Italian dining can be romantic. And there's also something romantic about a passing train. Put these together and you get a unique combination.
The copy, along with the good music and special sound effects, created a great radio commercial. And it was hugely successful. People would drive many miles, past dozens of Italian restaurants, to dine at this one because it was unique. And people respond to uniqueness.

Here's one more example of the impact of salience in creating advertising messages. The owner of a drug abuse clinic called me one day. He'd been running television ads soliciting patients. It was a very worthy company, but they weren't getting enough patients from the television ads to continue the expense.

I looked at their commercials. They were expensive, well-produced spots showing a guy who had just come out of rehabilitation. He stood there, with his wife and small daughter sitting next to him, thanking the company for saving his life and bringing his family back. It was very touching, with heart-tugging music. It was one of those emotional, appealing ads that struck a nerve in most people. But it didn't work.

So I started using a little AdSense. Who is the salient audience? It is someone who is addicted to drugs or alcohol. How can we define that audience? It's tough. Addictive people come in different ages, many races, and in both sexes. There are rich addictive people and poor addictive people. Some are homeless; some have a wife and three kids in high school. They're all entirely different. So what do they have in common, other than their addiction? Ask a psychologist. They will tell you. The one salient commonality is denial.

The reason it's not easy to quit an addiction is that the person denies he or she has a problem. It's the common element of alcoholics. It's the common element of drug abusers. Otherwise, if they knew the dangers, they would probably quit. Look at all the evidence over the years that cigarette smoking can affect your health. Then look at all the smokers. "Cancer won't strike me," they say. That's denial.

So if I'm addressing a drug addict with a message that suggests, "I can help break your drug addiction" they won't respond if they don't think they're addicted. And alcoholics don't think they're addicted. To be effective, the message must break through that denial. If you can't do that, you're spinning your wheels and wasting your money on precious, emotional messages. You might win a few creative awards, but you won't get patients.

My messages focused on the denial. One message was a close-up shot of a guy appearing to be sitting on the edge of a bed in a drab room. He looked like he had a really bad night, as he sat there in his dirty pajamas. He was looking right into the camera.

> "I'm O.K., man, I just had a late night, a rough night. But I'll be O.K." Pause. "What's that? Drugs?" a voice asks him.
> "Well, yeah, I did some. But I'm O.K. I know when to quit. My wife? Well, she left...but...she'll be back, man. She knows I'll quit." "Hey, I don't need to tell you anything man," he shouts! "I'm going to bed!" The camera zooms out, revealing the man lying in an open coffin. As he lay back, he slams the coffin shut. On the screen are the words: "You may be closer than you think."

Sound a little over-dramatic? Well maybe for you. You're not addicted. But to cut through denial, you have to get personal. And you have to be shocking. It worked. The campaign focused entirely on denial and its consequences and ended with a gentle suggestion that my client's organization was there to help. The organization helped a lot of

Salience has an enormous impact on any advertising campaign. This new way of thinking, this AdSense, should be the cornerstone of the micro-advertisers marketing plan.

I am one who believes that one of the greatest dangers of advertising is not that of misleading people, but that of boring them to death!

~Leo Burnett

Chapter Twelve
Get Your Head Out of Your Ads

There's another important obstacle to advertising success. It creates waste in the millions of dollars. And it's produced some of the most offensive, ridiculous, unappealing ads in history. It is the ego.

One day a radio sales rep told me an all-too-familiar story. On the previous day, she met a potential client, a plastic surgeon, who had called her station inquiring about ad rates. He spent the first fifteen minutes of the conversation crying the blues over how much money he had wasted on advertising.

He bought expensive four-color magazine ads and got absolutely no response. He tried newspaper advertising. He got some response, but not nearly enough to cover the cost. He spent money on cable television, to no avail. "Please," he implored. "I'm at my wits end. I can't afford to lose any more money!"

My sales rep, knowing that I could help the frustrated physician, made a suggestion. "Let me recommend someone who might be able to help guide you. An advertising consultant named Kirk Donovan."

Instantly, he responded with a dogmatic air. "I don't need help. No one knows my business better than I do. I'm not going to pay someone to do something I can do myself for free."

What he was referring to was the fact that most media offer a 15% discount if the advertiser places the business through an advertising agency. They do that because there's less work for the media salesperson to do since the agency does all the work. And the media wants more of the agency business. Most agencies handle more than just one account, so they develop "buying power."

Unfortunately, some media will use the 15% discount as a "hook" to close a potential client, even if they don't use an agency. This physician always did the advertising work and was always offered the discount.

Why pay that money to someone else when he can pocket it? More about the 15% myth in the next chapter.

He needed to get new patients. He called the radio station as a first step. And he obviously didn't know what he was doing, or the physician wouldn't have complained about all the money he wasted.

What is it people think they can be successful with advertising with absolutely no knowledge about advertising? No knowledge about the language of advertising. No knowledge about how to write copy that works. No knowledge of the methods and skills of media buying.

I know owners of big businesses who spend thousands of dollars a month on expensive accountants. These highly experienced, highly competent CPAs know exactly what to do to keep their client's taxes at a minimum and his investments yielding the maximum.

That same business owner will spend thousands of dollars on corporate attorneys who are well educated and adept at protecting their client's legal interests.

Then these astute business owners will spend $50,000 a month on advertising. They will have their office assistants call the television stations to place the television buy! And this uneducated assistant will meet with media salespeople to negotiate rates. She may be a terrific person but does she know the language of advertising?

Then the business owner will write a script and use his dull, everyday voice to record the ad. Does he know the right word?

In the case of the stumped surgeon, the one who "thought he could", he finally stopped advertising altogether. He tried radio for one month and said it didn't work. When I heard this story, it prompted me to include a section in my lectures called "Get Your Head Out of Your Ads!" One of the primary reasons why 85% of all advertising is ineffective, or not as effective as it could be, is that a large number of people who are doing it shouldn't be!

I had a media buyer tell me one day that she always recommended to her clients to do radio advertising in the Spring. She took me outside and said, "See, look how beautiful it is out here! Everyone is listening to radio, not watching television." I suggested that she look at the research. If people aren't watching television in the Spring, why do all the networks use the Spring as one of their biggest rating periods? The numbers may drop off in the summer months, with all the re-runs, but even then the average loss of audience is only about 10%. But the cost of advertising in the summer is less, compensating for the difference.

A major obstacle to success in just about anything in life is the ego. Relationships fail because people are too stubborn to communicate. Who likes to say they are wrong? Egos have caused more than one ugly war. And egos waste millions of dollars each day in this country on advertising.

How many ads have you seen or heard that featured the owner or manager of the business in the ad? Of course, you hear it all the time. You see a guy on television who is stiff, inarticulate and almost frightened. You listen to a guy on the radio who sounds like he's reading to you.

I tried to consult with an attorney who had been doing personal injury television ads for many years. He told me he didn't need me to negotiate his media because he had a secretary who could do it just as well. I asked her if she knew the Atlanta daytime cost-per-point. She had no clue what a cost-per-point was. I asked if she knew how to read a media competitive report, monthly tabulations of television advertising in most major markets. The report shows every business that ran television advertising during a particular period. It shows how many commercials they ran, the times the spots ran, and even the programs in which they ran. It even shows the approximate amount of money they spent on the campaign. Pretty useful information for positioning yourself among the competition. She had no idea what a competitive report was. She had no concept of positioning. She knew as well as an "expert" how to negotiate media for her boss.

The fact is that the attorney just didn't want to pay the media commission. But he didn't realize that if negotiated properly, by someone other than his secretary, by someone who understands how to buy media, the 15% commission fee could have been neutralized. Getting 15% more commercials on the air neutralizes the commission fee.

Why is this so? Because most media rates are negotiable and knowledge is power. The more knowledge you have of the rates at any given time, the more negotiating power you have. The more knowledge you have of what your competition is doing, the more power you'll have in determining how to get your share of the business.

Another example I always use in my seminars are the owners and managers of car dealerships. I have known owners and managers who, however, managers that have no clue how to advertise properly litter the automobile industry. They will advertise on stations and programs that they watch, and the ones their friends watch.

When I sold radio advertising years ago, I met with a banker in Ft. Walton Beach. There were two radio stations in town, my top 40 station, and the beautiful music station. This car dealer, an older gentleman, didn't listen to my station. And he said none of his friends did either. I tried to point out that an older audience had already made up their minds about a banking choice, but young people who listened to my station had no allegiance to any banks, but would need to make decisions soon. As he insisted that my station wouldn't do him any good I kept looking at an enormous mounted bass on the wall above his desk. I finally congratulated him on his catch and asked him what he used for bait. He said, "a worm." Then I asked him if he liked eating worms. He looked at me like I was crazy. "No I don't eat worms!" he said. "Well," I said, "that fish did!"

If you are a business owner making decisions on where to spend your money you need to determine what your listeners will respond to, not what YOU will. That is part of the reason why so much advertising fails because we go after what appeals to us, not to our potential audience.

Radio and television usually have sports programming that comes at a premium price. The sales managers of these stations tell the sales staff to hit the car dealers because most of them like sports. They offer free tickets to sporting events, and the stations send out attractive sales reps to "get their attention".

I recently watched a men's basketball game on television and saw an ad for a local Kia dealership. According to data men's basketball has a low percentage of women viewers, but women are twice as likely to choose a Kia-branded vehicle as opposed to men. There is a lot of programming that appeals to women, but the owner of this dealership wanted to see his ads in the basketball games when he watched. After doing some research, I found out that he was the lowest ranked Kia dealership in the market out of 8 Kia dealers. Another example of the need to get your head out of your ads. But the condition is rampant in the local car dealer industry.

What happened to the attorney who thought he could? He no longer runs television ads. Several television stations have even sued him to recover their money! He should have kept his head out of his ads and turned it over to someone who knew what they were doing. He had to learn the hard way!

Ads are the cave art of the 20th Century.

~Marshall McLuhan

Chapter Thirteen
The 15% Myth

Negotiable media is a term referring to any media that has parameters in their pricing structure. For instance, a television station may show a price on their rate card of $1,000 for a 30-second ad. If I offer $800 for that ad, and there is availability or avail, the station may sell it to me.

The only problem is that if another business comes along between the time I bought the ad and when it runs and offers $900 for that same ad space, the chances are that my spot will be "bumped" for the higher offer.

Therein lies the negotiability of advertising. The skill for a good media buyer is in knowing, at any given time, where those parameters fall. It's a blend of being able to get a lower rate (but not to the point of losing the avail) and not prostituting the integrity of the station's rates.

Naturally, the advertising salesperson's job is to get the highest rate possible to look good for management but still keep it as low as possible for the potential client to make the purchase.

A good media salesperson is trained to know exactly how much his potential client understands about media buying. The less the buyer knows, the higher the rate will be. The buyer who knows the parameters of media rates buying negotiates better results.

These parameters change regularly. During the second and fourth quarters of the year, more advertisers want to be on the air. These, of course, are the Spring and Christmas buying seasons when national advertising increases and local advertisers spend most of their ad dollars. More demand means less supply and less negotiability.

Political seasons are tough for media buyers because Federal law dictates that the political advertisers get the lowest rate the station has offered for any day-part during the previous three months. More demand, less supply, less negotiability.

During the first and third quarters, stations do everything they can to sell ads. More supply, less demand, more negotiability. And of course the lower the ratings of a station, the lower the demand. That means more negotiability.

Many years ago, long before I started selling radio advertising, negotiable media began offering a 15% commission to local advertisers as a "hook." "Look," they would tell a potential client who is on the verge of buying. "If you sign the contract now, I'll give you the 15% discount. We'll call it an in-house agency discount.

The reduced rate, called an agency discount, is for advertising agencies or media buyers who do the work. Those agencies put together the ad schedules, create the commercials, and give it to the stations "ready to run." That means less work for the station's salespeople. That gives them more time to be on the street selling! It was worth the 15% discount for the media.

But once it became a "hook," it became the fatal blow to a lot of micro-advertisers. "Why pay an expert to do the placement when I can save the 15%?" As time went on more and more advertisers found out about the discount and began demanding it. "If the guy next door gets it, so should I! Now, I would say that over 50% of all local advertising nationwide is spent by the local business themselves, rather than utilizing the services of legitimate agency or consultant.

I can't count the number of times I lost a potential client because a radio or television station offered them a discount. And a huge percentage of those ran for just a few months, then stopped. The station got their money, the client got his discount, but the advertising didn't work because the person doing the ads didn't understand what they were doing.

Instead of paying a company which could probably do better creative and get better rates because of the combined buying power of all their clients, otherwise, astute business owners will "do it themselves" to save the 15%. For example, if you spend $10,000, you have the buying power of $10,000. But the agency might have a combined purchasing power of $100,000. Guess who has more negotiability? Businesses that try to save the 15% don't have their head in their wallets. They have their head in their ads!

When I taught classes at Florida State University, I used to tell my graduating students what I considered to be one of the most important things they could hear at this stage of their lives. I told them that four years of college didn't mean that they were educated. It only means that they are educable.

College won't make you successful in any business. Law school doesn't teach you how to be a lawyer. It just teaches you the language of the law. You have to take that knowledge and become a good lawyer or a bad lawyer, using your talents.

Medical school doesn't teach you how to be a doctor; it teaches you the language of medicine. Understanding the language of advertising is an important first step in using AdSense. Unfortunately, there are no requirements for being an advertising consultant. And because there are no enforceable codes governing ad agencies or consultants there are a lot of people out there representing themselves as "experts."

They are not experts. In every community there are huge numbers of people who get out of college, work a year or two selling for a local radio station or TV station and then open their doors as a "consultant."

I know a gentleman in Atlanta who worked for several years at a small newspaper, selling advertising. After about four years, he went to work for a small radio station selling ads. He did that for two years.

Then he came to me and asked my advice about him opening an agency of his own. He was excellent at selling ads but had very little experience writing ads. He knew nothing about television. He was a good talker and was an amiable guy. What right did he have to take $10,000 or more a month from some small business and with a clear conscience, give advice on how to spend it? He's taking a real gamble with a lot of money-money that isn't his! The loss does not sting the consultant, only the client.

It's like going to Las Vegas and gambling with a lot of money, losing every dime, and going home happy. Only it's worse. The poor guy whose money was just thrown away, paid the gambler to waste it!

HOW TO FIND THE RIGHT HELP

If you're going to spend money on advertising, you must either learn how to do it or hire someone who knows how to do it. Don't just think you know what you're doing. Look beyond your ego and make decisions based on skill and knowledge, even if the 15% commission is causing you to do it yourself. It's an illusion if you end up losing much more than the 15% offered.

And if you're hiring someone to help you with your advertising do a little research. Don't make your decision to hire someone based on how well you like them. That sounds ludicrous, but believe me, that's exactly why most consultants or agencies are hired.

If you hire an agency let them offer their advice and suggestions. Don't just hire them to facilitate the ideas you have. They might have better ideas or could embellish yours.

I'm reminded of the story of a business owner who calls three advertising agencies to solicit their help. He asks all three agencies the same opening question.
"What time is it?"
The first guy said, "It's 2:30."
"I'll get back to you," the inquiring business owner said.
The second guy said, "I'll have to do some research and call you back."
The third guy said, "What time would you like it to be?"
He was hired on the spot.

Find out how much experience the companies you are screening have in buying all media? How much is their buying power worth? How long have they had their current clients? What is their reputation with the media? What is their education level? And critically...what do they know about behavioral science?

If you want to have a chance of falling into the 15% of advertising that is successful, you must first get your head out of your ads. That is until, of course, your head is filled with the knowledge, skill, and experience necessary to make prudent decisions.

There is an old saying that there are three kinds of lies in advertising…...big lies, white lies, and statistics.

~Mark Twain

Chapter Fourteen
Statistical Science

The statistical science of advertising is the essence of the media business. It is the tool by which all media establish prices to charge for their services.

The size of a radio station's audience, for instance, is measured statistically by a rating company. If a station gets high ratings, it has a significant share of the radio audience. If it has low ratings, it doesn't have a big audience. More about radio later.

When I sold radio advertising early in my career, in a small Florida market, the ratings at my station fluctuated from good to mediocre. When the ratings were good, we were able to charge higher rates. But when ratings were lower, we would do everything we could to avoid mentioning ratings. "If you live by the ratings, you die by the ratings" was the edict.

I will give you a frame of reference by which rate decisions are based in most markets. Again, I'll use a radio station example. But first, let me explain that no micro-advertiser has enough money to reach everyone in their market every month. The best thing they can do is reach as many as they can efficiently. Unless you have enough money, you will always miss potential customers.

Let's assume there are ten radio stations in our sample market. National advertisers that want to penetrate our market will go to the top 2 or 3 stations to place their client's money. The decision to make these buys is usually made far away by people who never even listened to radio in that market. The ad agencies or media placement services decide where to place their ads by looking at the ratings.

So how does the station establish the rates it charges for commercials? First, the station decides how many commercials it wants to sell each hour. These are called avails, short for availabilities. Some stations call them units. Now, an hour is an hour, whether you're in New York City or Tallahassee, Florida. The average number of avails sold each hour is about 12 to 15 units, either 30 or 60 seconds. That means a minute in New York should cost a lot more than a minute in Tallahassee, simply because the audience is so much bigger.

The most simplified way of determining rate is by using a cost-per-thousand basis. In New York City, if your audience size at 10 o'clock in the morning is 1,500,000 people, and you want a $10 CPM or cost-per-thousand, that commercial would cost $15,000.

$$\$15,000 \div 1,500,000 = .01$$
$$.01 \times 1000 \ (CPM) = \$10 \ CPM$$

If a station in Tallahassee reaches an average of 8,000 people and you want a CPM of $10, the rate would be $80 for the commercial.

$$\$80 \div 8,000 = .01$$
$$.01 \times 1000 \ (CPM) = \$10 \ CPM$$

Therefore, you can achieve the same cost-per-thousand in Tallahassee as you can in New York City, although you reach a lot more people in New York City. It can be just as cost effective.

Because there are a fixed number of messages sold each hour radio and television rates are on a constant up-and-down fluctuation, based on supply and demand. The number of local avails is greater for the Number Six rated station than for the Number One rated radio station because national advertisers buy a bigger chunk of the total avails on the Number One Station. Therefore, the Number Six Station has a greater supply of avails. Local rates should be lower.

More businesses want to buy the Number One station because of its greater audience size. More demand means higher rates once the avails begin to diminish. These factors are important when analyzing the efficiency of most media buys statistically.

Some businesses buy advertising on the lowest rated stations because the prices are so much lower. On the top rated station, you may get five spots for the budget you have to spend. But on the lowest rated station, you may get 50 spots for the same price. That's 50 lines in the water. But remember, you have to be where the fish are.

There's another way to say this. If an ad falls in the forest and there is no one around to hear it, does it make a noise?

The statistical science of advertising is essential in determining whether or not you are being cost effective in your media placement. By determining audience sizes, and by learning the cost-per-thousands of other competing media, media can assign and justify rates.

Again, the higher the ratings or, the more people the media reaches, the higher the rates will be. It is that station's reward for doing so well. And in most cases, these stations can establish the cost-per-thousand for their market.

Now let's look at each of the major media. We will explore their strengths and weaknesses, and how each is statistically priced. You'll see how decisions are made in determining where billions of dollars are spent annually.

And you'll see that AdSense also plays a major role in the statistical science of advertising.

You can say the right thing about a product and nobody will listen. You've got to say it in a way that people will feel it in their gut. Because if they don't feel it, nothing will happen.

~William Bernbach

Chapter Fifteen
Outbound Marketing

As we mentioned in earlier chapters, the media revolution centered around the digital revolution. Today, what we now call "traditional outbound media" constitute yesterday's major media. But the landscape changed drastically with the cell phone and other electronic devices. Now people search online for what they want. That is why we call it "inbound media." When people go online to search for something they get a myriad of choices. Research shows that they will usually go to a name they have heard of before through traditional media. So today's traditional media drives digital media. Outbound marketing drives and supports inbound marketing. In the revolution, a lot of the major media was destroyed. Media that only a few short years or decades ago were huge revenue sources have disappeared. Media like the Yellow Pages are gone. People now search online for phone numbers and addresses. The newspaper industry, which until recently was the number one revenue source in major media, is practically non-existent. I used to sit around at a favorite breakfast restaurant and see an Atlanta Journal sitting on every table. Now I never see a newspaper, but I see people of all ages looking at their cell phone or tablet. Direct mail has diminished in popularity among advertisers. Print marketing became a lot less expensive when advertisers realized they could show their wares on a person's cell phone, which is always right in their hands, or within reach.

But outbound marketing is still dominant in forming people's opinions about products and services. Let me describe some of them now. The ones that are still dominant and the ones that are not as nearly dominant as they used to be.

Many a small thing has been made large by the right kind of advertising.
~Mark Twain

Late on the night on April 14, 1912, a young telegrapher sat at his post high atop Wannamaker's Department Store in New York City. He was listening to signals on his wireless. He picked up an incredible message. "S.S. Titanic ran into iceberg...sinking fast."

Reporters, relatives and the curious descended on the store to receive reports from the young man with the "wireless fist." For three days and nights, the young man stuck to his post. President Taft ordered all the other wireless on the East Coast off the air so that this channel would be free of interference.

The wireless operator was a young Russian immigrant of considerable talent, genius, and foresight. His name was David Sarnoff. The disaster established the reliability and importance of wireless. But much more happened as a result of that somber night.

Sarnoff spent countless hours thinking about the significance of that fateful event. If simple dot-dash signals could be transmitted over thousands of miles, why can't more complex signals be transmitted as well?

The vibrations of music were just such signals. Sarnoff proposed a "radio music box" and outlined a plan of development which he believed would make it a "household utility." On that momentous night of April 14, 1912, radio was born.

The future "General" David Sarnoff made broadcast history as a pioneer, and later, as founder and Chairman of NBC, the National Broadcasting Company. He built a distinguished career that spanned over a half-century.

I spent the first twelve years of my career in radio. Before that, my parents were radio veterans from the "Golden Days of Radio." For much of my early career, radio advertising baffled me. For some businesses, it was a costly mistake. For some, the return was much greater than the investment. I was perplexed. What was the secret of making radio advertising work?

It's obvious the audience is there. Almost every U.S. household has at least one radio, and the average American household has 5.9 sets. Within one week's time radio reaches 93% of all people age 12 and over. Over 265 million Americans over six years old listen to radio each week.

The problem with radio is that there are many choices other than traditional radio stations. There are, Sirius XM, I-Pods, Pandora, I-Tunes Radio, Spotify and many more. So even though radio listenership is still a major media it has diminished in effectiveness for the advertiser. The local stations still need to make money, so rates haven't come down, but listenership has come down. So many local advertisers, depending on the type of business, aren't getting nearly the return on investment as in year's past.

Radio is a selective medium. That means there are many different types of music or talk formats, differentiated program formats appealing to various consumer segments. The firm that measures these many radio audiences is called Arbitron Research Company.

By learning to read an Arbitron Research Report in your market you can determine a narrow age group, male or female-dominated audiences, and even lifestyles of audiences.

Other research companies, like Scarborough, measures everything from what kinds of cars an audience prefers to when their next refrigerator might be purchased.

So research tells us audience sizes. Now how does a station determine rates? First, they have to decide how much inventory they have to sell. Radio ads are sold as "units," primarily 30 or 60 seconds in length. These units are "day-parts". Any spots falling between 5:30 am and 10 am are in the morning drive day-part. Midday falls between 10 am and 3 pm, and the 3 pm to 7 pm day-part is called afternoon drive.

These terms came about in the 1960s when most people had only AM radios, and AM stations were "king." With the advent and eventual dominance, of FM signals more radios went into the workplace.

127

These stronger signals went through concrete and weren't affected by fluorescent lights. The new signals were the doom of AM radio. The once significant gap in audience size from morning to midday to afternoons narrowed considerably. In some cases, midday even gets higher ratings.

The other day-parts are nighttime, overnights and weekends. At most stations, they all experience sharp drops in audience size during these times.

Even though the gap has narrowed advertisers still desire morning and afternoon drive times the most. But how many minutes are there to sell during these coveted times?

If a radio station averages 12 minutes of advertising per hour, that means they have 96 minutes of "prime" advertising time over a period of eight hours. That leaves 192 additional minutes available to sell to advertisers for the remaining 16 hours of the day.

The job of a radio station sales manager is to sell as many total units as possible. Packages are suggested, usually consisting of spots in every day-part. During my radio advertising sales days, we were trained to say, "People who work during the night spend money too!" A sales manager has to convince advertisers creatively to spread their money around. That fills the holes. Sometimes they'll include "value-added" items to their packages. Remotes are live broadcasts from an advertiser's location. A popular disc jockey will show up, armed with free hats, T-shirts, food, and refreshments. They will urge people to get in their cars and come down to meet them.

So a station may offer a package which includes five morning drive spots, five midday spots, five afternoon drive spots, five nighttime spots and a remote broadcast, all for a specified amount of money.

Or the station may offer you the sponsorship of a morning traffic report. The price may be higher than regular morning drive rates, but it's justified since you get an additional "billboard." For example, this message is brought to you by Bob's Downtown Clothiers.

The question you must ask is "how much impact can value-added have?" If the purpose of advertising is to create an image by "keeping your name out there," then these short mentions are justified. But if each message has to be used to entice a response, it can't be easily done in the 5 to 10 seconds that comprise a billboard.

There are only two ways to use radio advertising successfully. The first is a strategic campaign. In this method, you should run a lot of commercials over a short period. A good strategic campaign would utilize about 25 to 30 ads over a period of one or two weeks.

The second way to do radio advertising is to run fewer spots, between 5 and 10 per week, over an extended period. This is called a maintenance schedule. In this campaign, the purpose is to just "keep your name out there." This is where realistic expectations come into play. If you're having a sale to get rid of a large inventory that needs to me moved, you'd probably discount the price and put a limit on the time in which the public can get the savings. This is creating an "urgency."

For instance, a furniture store may have twenty new rocking chairs at a savings of 20%. "But hurry...these rockers won't last long at this price, and this sale ends Saturday."

If this is your "hook," but you run just five commercials in one week to announce it, you probably won't get the kind of results you expect. A lot of businesses will do this, sell only a few rockers, and think that radio advertising doesn't work.

Using the same furniture store, if you run a maintenance, or institutional, message, without a hook, and run 25 spots in a week, you probably won't get good results either. The message should have a "call to action" if you expect an immediate response. Everyone is not shopping for furniture every day.

An institutional message has a goal of letting prospective furniture buyers know that when the time comes for them to look for furniture, they should remember your name. This is also called "branding." Steve Jobs, the founder of Apple, said "the chance to make a memory is the essence of brand marketing."

A strategic message says "even if you don't need furniture right now, this rocking chair at this price is hard to pass up." Advertising can satisfy the need of a consumer in short order if you offer the product they need, when they need it, and at a competitive price. But advertising can also create a need. It can make a person who never knew they needed a "widget" think they need that widget. Spontaneity produces a lot of revenue in this country, usually with lower priced objects.

Advertising campaigns have to rely on the frequency or the number of times a person hears your message. A person needs to hear your message up to 10 times before they will retain the information.

It is important to note that there is a big difference between listening and hearing. You usually have the radio on in your car. Your mind is in traffic, or what you have to do at work, or your date last night. The radio is loud, and you hear the commercials, but you aren't actively listening to the content of the message. But if you hear the same message several times, and something about the ad catches your interest, you may eventually listen to it.

Radio sales reps tell me all the time, based on the research, how many "listeners" they have in morning drive. I say that they don't have that many "listeners." They have that many "hearers." Listening requires conscious involvement. It is up to the creativity of the message to get them to listen. Even if you are listening to a message, though you aren't in the market for what the message offers, you still note the name of the company. If the time ever comes that you are in need of the product the company offers hopefully, you'll remember that company's name, but only if you have enough notations in your memory from their commercials. The chance of that happening depends on the consistency of the ad campaign over an extended period without becoming rhetorical or resilient.

Advertising also has to rely on reach, which equals how many different people hear your message each time your spot runs. A successful campaign uses a combination of reach and frequency. Unfortunately, it takes a considerable amount of money to get a satisfactory return. But the payoff could be profitable you choose the audience appropriately, and the message does what it is supposed to do. The question becomes "do you have enough money and time to wait for that payoff?"

What if you have a business on the north side of town and decide to run a radio schedule which reaches the entire town and beyond? Is it worth spending money on the entire marketplace, knowing that the only people who would potentially respond are in your area? It depends. First, are you the only business in town that offers what you do? If so people will drive across town to find you. But there are few businesses that hold exclusive rights to a product line.

For example, a small to medium size market might have 4 or 5 Ford dealers, but only one BMW dealer. If you want a BMW, you will drive as far as you have to. You'll only pass the other 4 Ford dealers if you think the one farthest from you has more inventory or lower prices.

Otherwise you have to determine if there are enough people in your area who can respond to your message to make it profitable. Or, and this sounds pretentious, put another location on the other side of town and share the ad costs. One of the reasons so many companies have multiple locations in major cities is to diffuse the advertising costs in a competitive marketplace. This synergistic concept paved the way for "chain stores."

The only problem is you might not have enough money to open another location. There have been many well-run businesses with excellent products or services that go bankrupt, losing to well-financed companies with inferior goods and/or services. Survival of the fittest is the nature of business.

The advantages of radio are numerous. A radio station usually reaches a large number of people. And among all major media, radio is the best at targeting particular audiences. If you're appealing to people over 50, there are usually only one or two stations that program to that demographic. You can target your message specifically to that group.

Another advantage to using radio is that just about everyone listens to it sometime during the day. And radio is probably the easiest media to use. Print and television ads are expensive to produce and time-consuming. It doesn't take that much time or money to produce a radio ad.

What are radio's disadvantages? Well, it's the only major media that people utilize while doing something else. When you're watching television, you're focused it. When you're looking at your cell phone or computer, you're focused on the screen in front of you. But when you're listening to the radio you're usually driving, focusing on traffic or the other people in the car speaking to you or you might be working. It does not hold your attention like the other media do. It doesn't have the selective visual impact of television or digital.

Another disadvantage is that if you have a broad customer base, you'll need to buy more than one station. That can get expensive. Most people listen to more than one station. Button pushers pass up the advertising and go to another "favorite" station to find music. Your potential audience decreases when the music goes off, and your message comes on.

So if you have a large enough budget radio is best used in conjunction with additional media. This is called a media mix. Redundancy is a blend of more than one sense. If you see something visually, then hear it, chances are greater that you'll remember the message. Whereas the future of traditional media is nebulous in the fast-changing environment of entertainment choices, radio isn't going anywhere. As the digital revolution continues to grow and influence our television habits and sources for news and information are being redirected. But most people will still use the radio alarm to wake up, listen to the traffic and weather reports, and listen while driving their cars.

How you utilize radio in your advertising plan will determine the potential for success or the heartache of failure.

Advertising is salesmanship in print. Its principles are the principles of salesmanship. The only purpose of advertising is to make sales.

~Claude Hopkins

NEWSPAPER ADVERTISING

It's sad that a major media source is dead. Although it is not buried. Newspapers still exist, even if it is online. And it still greatly influences millions of people. But those millions of individuals are usually over 50 or 60 years old and grew up with newspapers.

I had always heard that Benjamin Franklin was the first person to introduce advertising to the Americas. Actually, the concept of advertising had already been thriving in England since the 1600s.

The very first advertisement in English was written by a gentleman named William Claxton in 1477. He was trying to sell a new book of prayer that he had published in Westminster Abbey.

The earliest ads were posters and broadsides nailed to post offices and courthouses. But by the end of the American Revolution advertising was here and already established. Even Paul Revere demonstrated skills of copyrighting in 1768 in an ad selling his brand of false teeth.

Whereas many Persons are so unfortunate as to lose their fore-teeth by Accident, and other ways, to their great detriment not only in looks but speaking both in Public and Private. This is to Inform all such, that they may have them replaced with artificial Ones that look as well as the Natural, and answers the End of Speaking to all Intents, by Paul Revere, Goldsmith, near the Head of Dr. Clarke's Wharf, Boston.

The first daily newspaper was published in Philadelphia, courtesy of a part-time printer named Benjamin Franklin. He was the first creative publisher to use pictures to break up blocks of copy. He was also the first to use a lot of white space around centered headlines. The first New York daily newspaper was begun in 1785.

During the first half of the Republic there was really no need to advertise. Most of the country lived on farms, where just about everything a family needed was produced. Householders sold what small surplus there was after the family met its needs. This surplus was the small amount of money the ads were appealing to. Most of it went for coffee, salt, hardware, clothes and tools. (Advertising in America, The First 200 Years, Harry N. Abrams, Inc., New York, 1990)

When economic conditions began to change, advertising as we know it began in earnest. Newspapers began to grow as we moved Westward to keep the new pioneers informed about what was going on back east. The age of Mass Communication began slowly and deliberately.

The use of newspapers for advertising went back generations and became ingrained in the American psyche. As the economy grew department stores, carrying everything a homeowner could wish for, began to sprout up. The only way these stores had to announce their wares was through newspaper advertising.

As early as 2016 there was about $23.5 billion spent on newspaper advertising. By comparison, there was about $17 billion spend on radio, $67 billion spent on digital and $81 billion spent on television.

So what about your business? When you're spending your money to try to move an audience to action one of the first things you should look at is the credibility of the medium. Newspapers, being centuries old, have a proven reputation for reliability.

As the Communication Age progressed people's hunger for information increased. Rather than wait weeks or months to receive information, our information now comes through the newspaper in detail the next day, or in some cases, the day the event occurs.

But the demise of the newspaper came at the hands of the digital revolution. Whereas people could read the details about a major event in the newspaper, they could only read it the next day. With digital they can read about is as it happens.

So, what are the advantages of this storied medium to the advertiser? Should you consider it in your advertising mix? Is it as profitable as it used to be? How big a gamble is it? And does it work better for some types of business than others?

The first thing that newspaper advertising offers is a mass audience, but mostly of seniors. Among its loyal readers, it enjoys a high degree of familiarity, acceptance, and respect.

Another thing that makes newspaper advertising a solid choice is that you can carry a picture of your product or service. It is a tangible medium. Ads and coupons can be cut out and brought to the advertisers so they can see the result of the expenditure.

And the audience who reads the newspaper is as varied as our lifestyles. The average entrepreneur will try to check the business page on a regular basis to see what his competitors are doing, to watch for trends in the ever-changing economy and to check investments.

The average American tries to keep up on world events and local events. Whereas radio and television give the audience a capsule of events, the newspaper can describe the event in more detail.

The global community and mass communication created in our society a desire to be the best, the fastest, the strongest, the most agile. And if we can't achieve these things individually we idolize the people who can. This hunger for success manifested itself into a huge industry...the sports business.

The Sports Page attracts people who can't watch each game or attend each event they desire but have a passion to find out if their favorite team won. And they want to discern every statistic imaginable on their favorite team. Even people who don't read the newspaper as much as they used to will pick up the local sports page to see the details of their favorite team's statistics.

Automobile, real estate, job employment and classified ads have individual sections in most newspapers, although they aren't nearly as prominent a source as they used to be. And the need for knowing what is happening with our neighbors and friends created the Social Pages. And of course, our opinions are shaped by essays on the Editorial Pages.

By attracting such a diverse audience newspaper advertising could target its salient audiences with more precision and better results. But could the advancement of mass communication contribute to the possible demise of the vehicle that began it all?

Newspaper circulation is decreasing in our society. Today's modern family has less time to read the paper than our ancestors did. Since the 1980s, American newspapers began going out of business as fast as Mom & Pop restaurants.

Once, most large American cities had both a morning and afternoon edition. Today, the afternoon editions are rare. According to the Radio Advertising Bureau, a typical reader spends less than 20 minutes with the newspaper. That will give you barely enough time to read the sections you want, much less spend time looking at the ads.

Along with decreasing circulation newspaper rates have continued to increase, due to the increasing costs of paper, production, and delivery. But it still commands a significant share of the total advertising expenditures. The popularity of this medium has created a great clutter of ads. The average advertising content today is 62% for a daily newspaper and 68% on Sunday.

So the enterprising newspaper sales representative will try to sell you a larger ad to "stand out." The problem is that larger ads don't always deliver enough of an increase in reach to justify the increase in cost.

Another disadvantage of newspaper advertising is that most newspapers offer little in the way of competitive separation, giving a distinct sales advantage to the advertiser who can provide the better price.

In addition, one of the primary targets for most advertisers, the 18-34 consumers, seldom looks at the daily newspaper. Studies show that they are much more prone to get their information from electronic media.

A great disadvantage to the advertiser is something the newspapers sell as an advantage. If you're trying to advertise just one time, the rate you are charged is called an "open rate." It's the most expensive rate in the newspaper. In order to get a better rate; you have to agree to a long-term contract, or a commitment to a large number of inches over a period of time, usually a year.

But what if the ad doesn't work. What if the expense of running the ad isn't covered by the results you get from the ad? You're stuck with a long-term contract. And if you don't live up to your original commitment, you are "short rated." The newspaper will go back to the original rate you would have been charged had you run a shorter commitment, and you will owe them the difference. Bad enough it didn't work, now you have to shell out more money!

I've seen many businesses suffer over the years because their newspaper advertising didn't work, and they were obligated for more money.

Automobile advertising used to make up a great amount of newspaper revenue. Our society has been trained over the years to go to the classified section of our newspaper to compare prices and see what local dealers have to offer. But again, with the digital revolution the number of pages of car advertisers in most newspapers is almost non-existent.

As of this writing, a full- page color ad in the local newspaper of a major city, without a contract commitment, would cost about $20,000 or more. If a dealer signs a contract that he will run that ad once or twice a week for a year, the cost of the same ad could get as low as $9000. Quite a difference!

But even with a low contract rate the ad that costs $,9000 would have to result in selling nearly 50 cars to make it a worthwhile investment. The ad comes out one day, and the dealer must sell 50 cars in that day to be profitable. Imagine how many cars the dealer would have to sell with a $20,000 ad. It would be almost impossible to be successful.

Take into consideration that market conditions change constantly, weather factors can create a successful or unsuccessful sales day, or that a competing dealer might have an ad right next to yours one day with lower prices on every car. That day would probably be considered a loss.

So what type of advertisers should be in the newspaper? How do you increase your chances for success? There are categories of business that have traditionally advertised in the newspaper, such as the aforementioned automobile advertiser.

One of the first categories were department stores. John Wannamaker's Department Store in New York City built its success with newspaper ads. Even back then, in the early 1900s, he stated that half of his advertising worked and half didn't!

Department stores of today have dominated newspaper advertising. to follow the tradition. Just look at the full page ads announcing a "White Sale" at your local department store. Most newspapers are full of them at least one day a week, if not more. Tires and auto parts have probably always been advertised in the Sports Page of your local newspaper on Saturday, because men buy tires and auto parts, and men will spend more time on the Sports Page.

Furniture stores have found newspaper pages to be very effective to announce their wares, especially since they can show pictures. And of course grocery stores have a long tradition of newspaper advertising although that has diminished greatly too with the advent of sources like Groupon.

As electronic communication and technology continues to advance, and as our society continues to offer other choices to get our information in a time-limited environment, the newspaper industry must find other ways to make their advertising costs more effective. I'm not sure how long newspapers will always be around, but the success of the industry in dominating advertising expenditures has suffered greatly.

Television will enormously enlarge the eye's range, and, like radio, will advertise to the Elsewhere.

~E.B. White—1938 lecture

TELEVISION ADVERTISING

There is much debate over who invented television. The beginning of the 20th century was a time when the brilliant minds of scientific discovery prospered. Alexander Graham Bell had recently invented the telephone. Guglielmo Marconi astonished the skeptics in 1899 by receiving the first radio signal –the letter "S" – in Newfoundland. The signal was sent from the other side of the Atlantic.

Thomas Edison continued to amaze the world with his inventions— the electric light bulb, the phonograph, the box camera and pictures with motion.

An article in the New York Daily News in early 1904 reported that a German scientist, Professor Arthur Korn, talked "very modestly of 'televista,'" the name he had given his 'seeing by wire' invention. The word television comes from the ancient Greek and Latin roots for "far off" and "see."

The article read, "Now that the photo-telegraph is on the eve of being introduced into general practice we are informed of some similar inventions in the same field, all of which tend to achieve some step toward the solution of the problem of television."

Dr. Korn had transmitted a photograph by way of a telegraphic circuit.

In 1884 a 24 year-old German inventor, Paul Nipkow, had shown that television was feasible. He devised a perforated disc through which images could be scanned by mechanical means; a rotating wheel that first broke down and then reconstructed the image.

In the early 1920s, while radio began to flourish, experiments continued in the effort of marrying sound and vision.

John Logie Baird, a Scottish tinkerer in the field of electronics, transmitted the first moving image...shades of light and shade barely recognizable as a face. His apparatus was adopted by the Germans and the young British Broadcasting Company, or the BBC. Many believe that his early work qualifies him for the title of the "inventor" of television.

Meanwhile in the United States, Charles Francis Jenkins was doing similar work. As early as 1923 he transmitted a picture of President Warren G. Harding by wireless from Washington D.C. to Philadelphia, Pennsylvania.

In 1924, at a farm in Idaho, a young man named Philo Taylor Farnsworth had worked out the concepts of a television system. His first application for a patent for his "cathode ray tube" was made on January 7, 1927.

These were the pioneers of television. The first commercial television station, WNBT in New York, began broadcasts to about 4,700 TV set owners in 1941. Less than 50 years later there were over 1,250 television stations and 830 cable systems in the United States. Today those numbers shrink in comparison.

Today television has overtaken all other forms of media in its power and impact. In the 1940s families would sit down with their favorite beverage and stare at their radio with undivided attention. Do they do that today?

Television, with its sight and sound and motion, is the most intrusive form of media today. Every radio station has its own distinct audience demographics, but a television station reaches every conceivable demographic during the course of a day.

The sources for the micro-advertiser's advertising expenditures on television can be broken down into two categories. The first is the local over-the-air network affiliates and independent commercial channels. The second method is to use local cable channels.

Network affiliates usually have the largest audiences. These stations carry network programming during the most viewed day-parts, usually comprising of early morning new programs, dinnertime news hours and the "prime time" period of 8 p.m. until 11 p.m.

During these high profile times the station receives and transmits signals originating from network headquarters. Each program has a certain number of local availabilities, called "local breaks." These are obviously the most expensive spots available on the station because there are so few of them and they reach the largest number of people.

The cost of a spot in these areas can reach into thousands of dollars, which makes it unaffordable to many micro-advertisers. These spots are usually purchased by the businesses that group together their ad budgets. For instance, a local Dodge dealer can't afford a prime time spot, but the Dodge dealer group, with much deeper pockets can afford it. A single restaurant may not be able to afford these time slots, but a franchise group of dozens of restaurants can afford it.

The micro-advertiser basically "fills in the holes." These time slots don't reach nearly as many people as prime time, but even smaller television audiences can have a lot of impact. These advertisers can't afford to buy time on the National news but may be able to get a spot in the six p.m. and 11 p.m. local newscasts.

There are plenty of availabilities during the daytime, late night and weekend programming. These are the areas where television stations realize huge profits.

Independent stations have a great deal more time to sell than local network stations. These stations carry scarce, if any, national programming. They show an abundance of sitcom reruns, specials, and movies.

Whereas a network station might offer 7 or 8 local avails during the nine p.m. until ten p.m. period, an independent station with no national time slots could sell up to 20 commercials to local advertisers during the same period. With a larger supply of avails on an independent station, the rates can be more affordable to the small advertiser.

High profile cable stations are another source of advertising. The stations list as: CNN, Fox News, and other information channels, the A&E's, the Discovery Channels, the History Channels, the Lifetime Channels, the music channels like MTV and VH-1, the children's channels like Nickelodeon and The Cartoon Network, the classic movie channels, the sports channels like ESPN and many more.

These networks and their enormous amount of avails can target a narrow group of demographics and lifestyles. The only problem is the small number of viewers these networks attract at any given time.

Even in prime time, these networks attract only a small sliver of the available audience. So if a local Kia dealer runs a cable ad, there is something vital to consider. Remember only 1% of the audience is in the market for a car on any given day. And Kia attracts only about 5% of automobile sales. That means that only 5% of 1% of the viewing audience would potentially respond to your commercial. What kind of impact could you expect by reaching 5% of 1% of a small sliver of the viewer? Your chances are rather slim.

How are ad costs determined? For a thirty-second spot on television, there are several determinants. The first is the size of the audience within your coverage area. The next determinant is the audience size for a particular station and a particular show.

Another determinant is the number of ads you buy over a period. It just makes sense that a station will charge a higher price to a client that buys one spot, as opposed to a 200 or 300 spot purchase. This is called "packaging." The advantage to the television station is to sell some of its ad slots in undesirable time periods. What it does for the advertiser is reduce the average cost per spot significantly.

Both the network stations and the cable stations define their core service by geography. This coverage area is called the Area of Dominant Influence, or ADI. Networks and most independent stations cover a larger area than most cable stations, but the advantage of cable is that it can target a more defined area. .

One cable provider can break down their advertiser's coverage by the community. Of course, the audience size diminishes significantly, but it is narrowed down to a particular geographical location. If you sell tires at a store that is located only on the north side of town, why would you want to reach people on the other side who have their own local tire stores?

How does a television station measure its audience size to determine rates? They do it by measuring terms like reach, frequency, rating and share. Here are some things you need to know when buying television advertising.

A station's rating or share is determined by independent survey firms. The best known of these firms is the Nielsen Research Company.

A rating is the audience size shown as a percentage of the total population. A rating point constitutes 1% of the households using television. The share of audience is usually expressed as a percentage of TVs that are tuned to a specific channel at a particular time out of all

TVs in the coverage area. For instance, a share of 15 simply means that 15% of the televisions in the market area are watching a particular channel at a given time.

Television audience potential is based on households using television, or HUT levels, and persons using television or PUT levels. These numbers show the number of televisions that are in use during a specific period.

Gross impressions are the total audience of average quarter hour persons available for the total number of commercials per any given schedule. Gross rating points (GRPs) are the total of all rating points gained for a given schedule.

Finally, there is cost per rating point and cost per thousand. CPR is the cost of reaching 1% of the population in a particular age group. Cost per thousand is the price of delivering 1000 gross impressions.

There are two other things to learn if you are trying to buy an effective media schedule. Frequency is the average number of times a person can see your commercial. Reach is the number of viewers who are expected to see an ad on a station in a given period, such as a week or a month. It is the unduplicated number of homes who might see the ad at least once.

So if an ad campaign exposes over 500,000 households in one week, and there is a net reach of 70,000 unduplicated households, your frequency would be 7.1. That means the average TV viewer will see your commercial 7.1 times over the week.

These numbers can be confusing and overwhelming to the television advertiser, but they are the only determinants available to gauge the price effectiveness of an ad campaign. You need to learn and understand and understand these terms. Don't act like you know it. Ask your media representatives to teach you.

T.V. ADVANTAGES

So what are the major advantages to television advertising? Since the digital revolution, most traditional media audience sizes have been eroded. But the only major media that has not taken a large hit is television. Somewhere in this country, just about every home has a television on sometime during the day or night. Television reaches large segments of your potential audience at the local level. Television is also unbeatable at appealing to the emotions. Television spots can combine sight, action, color and sound to leave an impression with impact.

There is also a certain aura of prestige that accompanies being seen on television if the message is properly portrayed.

Television offers advertisers the opportunity to reach limited demographic groups, enabling them to target their message to their potential audience. For instance, stock brokerage firms would reach a salient audience on Fox News, CNBC or MSNBC.

The disadvantages? Well, your chances of reaching a sizeable audience outside your market area are enormous because of television's reach.

If a micro advertiser can't afford to buy a lot of frequency, his message may get lost in the clutter of other ads. In many cases, TV advertising loses its impact if an advertiser cannot buy reach and frequency. You have to commit to a long-term campaign to see noticeable results.

Realistic expectations must come into play. If you can't afford frequency over a short period, you should expect to spend money over an extended period to see the success of your expenditure. Unfortunately, not a lot of small businesses can afford to spend that much money without seeing immediate results.

The production of the ad itself can be cost prohibitive. Some spots may cost thousands of dollars to produce, and that is before it even gets on the air!

One of the most frustrating advertising disadvantages was created by the invention of the remote control. All the ratings and shares of a particular program in a particular day-part mean nothing if the audience switches to another station during your commercial.

The explosion of programming choices and channel availability will continue to fragment television audiences. Technology and the advent of the computer will certainly change the landscape of television and will produce a smaller impact from your advertising dollars.

As Edward R. Murrow once said of television, "The instrument can teach, it can illuminate, yes it can even inspire. But it can do those things only to the extent that those humans are determined to use it to those ends. Otherwise, it is merely lights and wires in a box."

Will it increase your knowledge and understanding of the world around us? Or will it become the push-button opiate? As they say in television, "Tune in next week."

Twenty years ago your marketing effectiveness was a function of the width of your wallet. Today your marketing effectiveness is a function of the width of your brain!

~Brian Halligan and Dharmesh Shah

Chapter Sixteen
Inbound Marketing

What is inbound marketing? It a phrase coined in the new millennium, mostly attributed to a leader in digital marketing called HubSpot. They are a marketing software platform that helps companies attract new visitors, convert leads and close customers. Now an industry term, inbound marketing is basically what is called "permission-based" marketing. It is non-intrusive, because the audience has gone to their chosen mediums and given you permission to communicate with them. The other premise behind inbound marketing is to answer questions the public asks, and spread those answers around the web in anticipation of the question being asked by other people.

The audience at any given time is smaller than mass media audiences, but it is more accepting of the advice or suggestions you offer them. Types of media that fall under this permission based model are social media, blogs, webinars and other forms of distributing messages like email marketing.

Also your audience in permission based marketing can be reached more specifically by targeting keywords. By using keywords, you can answer any anticipated questions from your potential audience might be asking. This can be done through search engine optimization, content strategy and landing page strategy. The digital marketing company worth its weight constantly create new landing pages for your business and targeted to your industry.

So inbound marketing, simply, is an audience that is specifically searching for you, or someone in your industry or business, at any given time of day or night. They are reaching out to you. Now you just have to convince them that you are the person they should call. After all, there are very few businesses or services in your immediate area that don't have hundreds of competitors available on the web. The worldwide web introduces you to competitors from all over the world, not just competitors in your back yard.

Inbound marketing uses a lot of forms, including content marketing, social media, content marketing and more. Pull marketing is the approach used by companies to attract new customers, reinforce branding in current customers and strengthen awareness in the pursuit of creating a demand for their products or services. This is done through search engine optimization, or SEO.

The world has become an overload of information and a scarcity of attention. Information has to be quick and concise. People live in a frenzy trying to catch up and stay ahead. According to IBM, in 2015 90% of the data in the world had been created in just the last couple of years.

Inbound marketing can provide the consumer the answers they are searching for at the exact time they need it. When I was growing up in California the research we had to do for school came from libraries. There was an entire industry that sent door to door salespeople to every corner of America selling Encyclopedias. At that time my mother was the sole bread winner, and didn't make a lot of money. So she could only afford the A through M books. She said she would buy N through Z next year! Which she never did. Not sure how I got through school, but I remember not doing very well in nutrition through zoology!

Today all the information you need is at your fingertips. You just have to be in the mood and ready to push the buttons, and have the imagination to know how to search the right words that will get you to your destination. That is one of the things that has eroded traditional media, and in some cases destroyed it. Forrester Research wrote in 2013 that "today's buyers might be anywhere from 2/3 to 90% of the way through their journey before they will engage with a vendor's sales representative."

In other words, inbound marketing attracts customers to you so you don't have to chase them down.

What are the benefits of inbound marketing? There are many. It can create in the mind of the consumer a preference for a particular brand. That can influence future buying decisions.

It can generate social media shares and put customers in control. Inbound marketing can help fuel SEO efforts and help enforce brand awareness. It can be done any time of the day or night, not wait till your doors open. And most important to businesses, it can drive qualified leads for a lot less money than traditional advertising.

There are many kinds of inbound marketing, and none of them work effectively on their own. Most incorporate all, or parts, of the following elements.

SEARCH ENGINE OPTIMIZATION

SEO is a very important segment to inbound marketing. If you use the right key words, and have a good website with effective design, you will be in good shape to launch your company to the top of search results. That means you will be seen on the first page when someone types in your product or service in the search bar. For example, as of this writing, Google was the #1 search engine, providing for almost 12 billion searches a month. It gets 67.5% of the United States search market and 87.1% of the mobile search market. Why is that important? Because 93% of all buying decisions start with a search online.

The key is to get on the first page because those websites garner 91.5% of Google traffic. If you're on the second page you will only get 4.8% of the traffic. And page 3 only gets to 1.1%.

Content marketing in an integral part of SEO marketing. They are two different forms on marketing, but they have to work together to be effective. There are differences though. SEO demands content. Content marketing IS content. SEO demands keywords. Content marketing means using keywords. The only way you can use your keywords is to employ them strategically in your content on your website. Content marketing uses great content, written for humans, and utilizing the keywords that you are targeting. Your SEO campaign will surely fail if you don't integrate good content marketing. A professional digital marketing firm can guide you in the right direction.

SEARCH ENGINE MARKETING

Google AdWords is by far the leading network on the web. This is called SEM, or search engine marketing. Many people in the business call this form of marketing pay-per-click, or PPC advertising.

When someone is searching for a place to buy a new sofa they would probably type in the keyword "sofas". When the first page comes up you will usually see several advertisements at the top of the page. You know that because the word "ad" is the first thing you see. You will probably see 4 or 5 furniture companies having a big sale on sofas. Whenever someone clicks on one of those ads they will be connected to a website for that company buying the ad. Google charges a fee for every person who clicks. The company doesn't pay anything if no one clicks through to the website.

When you scroll down past the ads you will see listings for many other furniture companies. These show up as a result of SEO marketing. It doesn't cost anything when someone clicks on your site, except the money you spend on SEO marketing to keep your site on the first page.

Using AdWords requires time and money, but many businesses have determined that it is money well spent. The most appealing fact is that PPC delivers a measurable return on investment. But using SEM alone usually doesn't work. It can deliver immediate results, but your marketing efforts work best with a combination of SEO, SEM and traditional marketing. That is IF you can afford to do all of them.

Let's use online travel agencies as an example. Just about all of the revenue earned by these companies are derived through digital sources. That means people go online to book their travel and pay by credit card online. So why do these companies have to do traditional advertising?

The top 18 travel agencies spent many millions of dollars on digital advertising in 2015, but they spent over $625 million on traditional television advertising. One of the biggest of these firms, Travelocity, spent $14 million on television ads utilizing a cartoon character called the "roaming gnome".

One of the secrets of search engine advertising is that the money is made buying your own brand name. But the clicks are more expensive and the return is fairly low. So to get customers to search them by brand name, which is less expensive, Travelocity increased their television advertising expense. By doing this they captured a lot more market share. In 2015 they spent about half of its $100 million advertising budget on television ads. Brand search terms cost them about 20% of their ad budget but delivered nearly 80% of their return.

The online travel agencies are in a real dogfight. They are being dichotomized by individual travel sites like hotels or airlines and their share is being eroded. They struggle for differentiation and trying to create loyalty, which is very difficult. That is where the creative becomes important, like the use of the cute gnome. Search activity is driven by interest generated in other media, and television commercials drive search usage more effectively than any other form of traditional media.

The other major online travel agencies are well known television advertisers. Expedia, Trip Advisor, Priceline, Hotels.com, Trivago, Orbitz, Hotwire...all are very recognizable television advertisers.

And it doesn't stop at travel agencies. Other companies that derive the lion's share of their revenue from online brand themselves through traditional media...companies like LegalZoom.com, Ancestry.com, Netflix.com, EHarmony.com, Match.com and Esurance.com. Where did you first hear about these companies? Through television branding.

Traditional media like television cannot quantify results like digital media can. It is much harder to determine a return on investment. But ask companies like Travelocity that cut their traditional media for a short time, saw their revenues decrease greatly, only to go back to spending huge television advertising dollars.

Traditional media drives digital media. Outbound marketing supports inbound marketing. With just digital media you stand among literally thousands of competitors with no names and no faces. When you have effectively branded your name and your image your name will stand out when people search online.

As I mentioned, as of this writing Google AdWords dominated the digital landscape in terms of search engine marketing, but there are still other choices. The other leading search engines are Yahoo and Bing. The rest are a mixed bag. Some search engines are focused on social media, others give access to a diverse blogging audience, but the problem with most of them is traffic quality.

SOCIAL MEDIA

Over 2/3 of online adults use social media to share information. Companies like Facebook, Twitter and Pinterest became household names in just a matter of a few years.

One of the largest of these at the beginning of the 21st Century is a company started by Mark Zuckerberg in his dorm room at Harvard University. It took the social media world by storm, and is utilized by toddlers to grandmothers. The problem that arises, and will eventually weaken the strength of the medium, is the younger generation. How long will they stay on Facebook when their mother or grandmother "friends" them. Privacy is tantamount to everyone, young and old. How willing will we be to share our social values with people who we don't want to know what we do in our private lives?

Google+ is a clean and simple interface, which makes connecting with friends, family and business associates easy. When it started it became the fastest growing social network in history.

Twitter came along and became a widely used tool for everything from business to fun and games. And its power became evident during the 2016 Presidential campaign in the United States. It became a high profile network when in 2014 President Barack Obama became the first American President to sign on and give his first "tweet" using the handle @POTUS. From the outspoken Donald Trump to Bernie Sanders every major candidate devoted a team of staff devoted to reaching as many people as possible using this method of name recognition. It became as important as traditional media, and in some cases more important.

For instance, Donald Trump changed the way political campaigns use social media. Using a combination of large rallies, social media and traditional media he surged to the top of the Republican ticket without having the advantage of past political experience. By using brash and inflammatory commentary on Twitter he was able to spend much less money on traditional media than any other candidate.

By the end of his successful campaign he amassed 9 million followers on Twitter. By comparison each of the major TV news networks, ABC, NBC and CBS, only had about 7.2 million viewers on an average evening newscast. Using this 140-character medium of Twitter he commanded a much larger audience than the traditional powerhouse TV networks. His sound-bytes were short but effective.

And an elderly socialist politician named Bernie Sanders commanded a huge youthful following by promising free college and other social issues that appealed to them. With an average of 2,000 retweets per hour he became a social media powerhouse. His pop-culture appeal and his ability to inspire people to create their own social media content around him he became one of the most fascinating storylines of the campaign. It wasn't enough to win, but it was enough to show the world the power of social media.

Social media is authentic and sentimental, has a huge reach, engages its audience like no other medium in history and has had a huge impact on the world around us. Of course the digital world has many other sources of information and entertainment. Blogging, discussion boards and forums, Email marketing, MySpace, Picasa, iTunes and many more.

Other social media platforms the fast growing Instagram, the business oriented LinkedIn, MyLife, Friendster, Blab, Flickr and many more. Who knows what power and influence they will have in years to come, but as the digital revolution shows the world is fickle. What was hugely popular today can be in the dust bin of digital graveyards tomorrow.

But how long will social media, in its present form, survive? I have heard many horror stories about families feuding over posts on social media. Most of the fights are trite, like "why didn't you include me in your birthday party plans?" or "you put a lot of pictures up but I didn't see any pictures of me!"

The hazard of utilizing social media is that it is highly intrusive. The first big social media platform as Facebook. But after several years, young people were getting criticized by parents for posts they saw on Facebook, so many of them strayed to other methods of communication like Instagram and Twitter. What affect will social media have on the American family? What will this pathway to people around the world do to personal social interaction? The impact of social media changes every day with the introduction of new platforms of communicating. Whether those changes are positive or negative will only be determined by history.

In summation, today's businesses have realized that traditional outbound efforts alone aren't enough to produce profits and stay in the forefront of the consumer's mind. Inbound marketing techniques need to be utilized to attract more leads and enforce brand awareness and trust. Businesses need to introduce a disciplined approach to content creation, introduce marketing automation tools that can help them nurture and score leads, and optimize how these leads flow through the sales pipeline.

*Promise, large promise, is the soul
of an advertisement.*

~Samuel Johnson

Chapter Seventeen
Paralinguistics

Working on my Master's Degree and Doctoral coursework at Florida State University, I taught a course called Nonverbal Communication. We don't start speaking until we are over a year, almost two years old. But we start communicating nonverbally the minute we're born. Ever see a baby smile? Who taught the baby that? Nonverbal communication is innate, not learned. It incorporates the way we smile, the way we walk, the way we dress, the way we use eye contact, the way we use facial expressions, our body language and more. We communicate nonverbally over 80% of the time, but we only communicate verbally about 15% of the time. Our educational system in built around verbal communication, not nonverbal communication. I knew from the beginning of my coursework how important nonverbal communication is for success, happiness, relationships and so many other facets of life. Through my studies and teaching, I created my book "Where Did the Love Go?", a look at nonverbal communication in infatuation and relationships.

A form of nonverbal communication that is salient to advertising is called paralinguistics. Paralinguistics is not WHAT you say, it's the WAY to say it. That is a critical ingredient in broadcast, both radio, and television, to create credibility and believability. This chapter will highlight the necessity of using proper paralinguistics in the delivery of a message.

I was listening to a radio ad for a car dealer one day and heard the announcer say, "And you keep rebate!"

And you keep rebate?! When you look at internet ads you've probably seen this expressed in a starburst with the words, "You keep rebate!" Some radio station announcer had the assignment to write an ad for the car dealer. He looked at the dealer's website for copy points. I know. I spent my early radio career doing just that.

When the announcer saw, "You keep rebate," he wrote it into his script. But if you were speaking to someone you would say, "You keep the rebates." This announcer isn't speaking to you. He's reading to you.

It's difficult enough for your ad to stand out among the clutter of other canned ads, disc jockeys' ramblings and all the other noise on a radio or television station without hearing someone read to you.

Let me reiterate one important point. No one turns on the radio to listen to commercials. Aside from the Super Bowl telecasts, no one turns on the television to watch the ads. We don't like to be the recipients of advertising messages.

Advertisers spend real money for their ads to be heard or seen. Your ad has to cut through the clutter.

Remember there's a great difference between "hearing" and "listening." You "hear" auditory sounds. "Listening" requires your attention and possible retention.

If you hear an ad that sounds like someone is reading to you what do you think are the chances for you to be drawn to attention? The odds are greatly diminished.

Why does the announcer in our example sound like he is reading to you? Because he is reading to you! A script is a series of words and thoughts that have been written down on a sheet of paper.

This is very important. We write as we read and we read like we write, but we don't speak like we read or write. "You keep rebate" was written down for someone to read it. But we wouldn't say it to someone that way.

If you speak words that have been written, you sound like you are reading. It's only natural. But how do good announcers read scripts and make them sound as if they're making the words up as they go? It's with the understanding of paralinguistics.

Paralinguistics is a form of nonverbal communication that has to do with the way words and thoughts are spoken.

There's nothing more annoying than having an ad read "at" you. Take situations in which two people are talking to each other leading up to the "sell" of the product they are advertising. Read them out loud as you go, like you are reading from a book.

> "Honey," the man says. "I think we should get out
> of the house this weekend."
> "O.K. Where do you want to go?"
> "Well, I heard about a great new restaurant. It is
> called Angelo's. They have great food."
> "Great food! That's what I'm in the mood for. What
> a great idea!"

Pretty lame. But you hear ads like this all the time. Would you speak to your spouse like that?

And if the script wasn't bad enough, the people using the script are reading to you.

So how can paralinguistics help? We speak using a language different than our written vocabulary. Our spoken language is filled with slang, dialect, and non-fluencies.

Slang is a nonstandard vocabulary of a culture or subculture, consisting of figures of speech marked by spontaneity. In the South, we say "ya'll." Up North, we say "youse guys." A dialect is a regional variety of a language distinguished by pronunciation, grammar or vocabulary.

A non-fluency is a nonverbal communication term referring to a stutter, a pause or a repetition of words. Non-fluencies are the natural methods by which we express our thoughts in words.

We use non-fluencies in our speech constantly. For instance, a script could be written as follows:

"Weekends are for enjoyment. You work hard all week. Why not take the family out this weekend for boating, biking, fishing or picnicking at Lake Lanier Resort?"

That seems easy to read. It sounds like something you'd read on a brochure. Now, make it sound like you're making it up as you go, adding non-fluencies. "Ya know, weekends are for enjoyment." "Ya know" is a non-fluency, something you added to personalize the statement...like "yeah" instead of "yes."

"Why not take the family out this weekend for boating...(pause)... biking...(pause)...fishing...(pause)...even   picnicking...(pause)...at Lake Lanier Resort?"

In writing, and when we read, we're taught that a comma is a signal to pause. A period is a signal to stop. But when we speak we can ignore these principles.

Read this out loud:

> "Imagine seeing the world through the wide window of an Amtrak Train. Relax as you watch tremendous mountains and gentle streams as you pass by. Explore cities so big and beautiful they take your breath away!"

Now, follow the way we would probably "say" these lines like you're making them up as you go.

> "Imagine...(pause)...seeing the world through the wide window...(pause)...of an Amtrak Train.   Relax... (pause)...as you see tremendous mountains...(pause)... and gentle streams as you pass by...(pause)...and explore cities and towns and sights so big and beautiful...(pause)...they...(pause)...take...(pause)... your...(pause)...breath away!"

There's a lot of pauses where we see no commas and even a place where we continue when we've seen a period. It's O.K. It's paralinguistics.

I'll continue to use this Amtrak copy to help you through but first, let me describe some things you need to know about paralinguistics.

Paralinguistics requires good voice and diction. A good voice is clear, resonant, and has adequate breath control. It has a clear, understandable rate of speech and an appropriate pitch level.

Articulation means we are producing individual sounds clearly. Enunciation produces linked sounds clearly, as in words. Diction means we are producing both sounds and ideas clearly.

Paralinguistics is how we use things like articulation, pitch, loudness, rate and quality of voice and diction to communicate messages beyond words and sentences.

Vocal qualities have been proven to indicate our moods, our attitudes, our state of health, even our self-esteem.

It's said that lasting first impressions are formed within minutes of an encounter. When a listener can't see all the nonverbal characteristics that make up credibility, when the voice is the only qualifier of these first impressions, it is mandatory that the voice uses proper paralinguistics to identify that credibility.

One of the important elements of good speech is pitch. Pitch has to do with changing voice levels as you speak. The pitch of your voice helps determine the meaning behind your words.

Take a word as simple as "yes." Let me ask you a question: Would you like to go?

Now answer out loud saying the word "yes" as if you really do want to go.

Now say it as if you will go, but don't really care one way or another.

Now say it like you really don't want to go, but I have bullied you into it.

Hear the pitch change?

> Try this exercise now. Say the words, "I didn't do that."
> Say it first like you would normally say it, sort of matter-of-fact in your delivery. "I didn't do that."
>
> Now say it defensively, like I've accused you of it before. "I didn't do that!"
>
> Now say it like you are angry for bringing it up again. "I didn't do that!"

An argumentative tone of voice is emphasized by using accentuated elements of pitch.

Loudness is another form of paralinguistics, which can indicate mood or create tension. Loudness is the perception or the degree of force with which a sound is produced.

First speak each of these sentences softly. Then, using the underlined words, increase loudness.

> Don't do that.
> Leave me alone.
> Give it to me.
> Get out of here.
> I love you.

See how loudness can affect meaning, sincerity, sarcasm or emphasis.

Non-fluencies are also used in the rate of speech. The rate is the number of words per minute one speaks.

Speech phrasing is forming a group of spoken words that constitute a meaningful unit and is surrounded by pauses. If someone speaks too fast, they lose credibility. The same holds true if someone is hesitant in his or her speech.

Syllabic stress is the emphasis on a given syllable.

Let's go back to our Amtrak script. When we write words like "big" and "beautiful," we know the impact of those words in our mind. But when we read the words out loud we just say the words.

As an instructor in paralinguistics for over 15 years at the Atlanta Broadcast Institute, I had hundreds of people with good voices read the Amtrak script. In almost all cases they said the word "big" the same way they said the word "beautiful."

But there is a significant difference between the words.

Take the time to say these words like they are imagined. "Big" is BIG! You stretch the "I" and you say it with force.

The word beautiful is very different. You speak it softer and more deliberately. "Beau-ti-ful." You stretch the letters "beau" and say it softly.

Write these words on a sheet of paper and ask someone to read them. I'll bet they will say each word using the same emphasis. That's because they are reading words that have been written down. Now, get them to express the words. See the difference?

Now say these words using extenuated rate of speech, proper pitch, and stressing the loudness or softness of the words. I'll write it down the way you would say it rather than the way you would read it. Sometimes that helps when writing a script.

"Imagine...seeing the world through the wide (stress the "i") window of an Amtrak Train. Relax...as you see tremendous (stress "men") mountains...and gentle (softly) streams as you pass by. And explore cities and towns and sights so big (say it big) and beautiful (say it with meaning) ... they... take...your breath away."

Notice how the rate of speech changes at the end of the sentence. We slow it down to increase the impact of the statement.

Try saying the word "breath" using only your breath, like it was meant to be said. The words "they take your" and "away" can be said with normal loudness, although emphasized individually. When you get to the word breath, drop your loudness and almost whisper the word, making it breathy.

THE POWER OF PARALINGUISTICS

What is the power of paralinguistics? Can you describe someone who has "personality" using only nonverbal signals? How about someone with "charisma?" A lot of their charisma comes from their voice.

What are the voice elements of someone who is confident or credible? What do you think when you hear someone with a "smiling" voice? You probably like them right away.

Can you tell when someone is "talking down" to you? Their sentences end on a down note or an abrupt note. They display the negative elements of paralinguistics. I can't believe the number of businesses I telephone that have a receptionist who sounds as if my phone call is a real burden. Companies, who spend untold amounts of advertising dollars telling people they are friendly and credible, have receptionists (who offer the first impression of the company) sound unfriendly, even downright nasty. These companies don't understand the importance of paralinguistics in communication.

When you run a radio or television ad, it isn't enough to write salient copy. And it isn't enough to just place your ad right in front of your potential audience. The copy needs to be delivered comfortably, confidently, in a relaxed pattern of communication that we're used to hearing when we are listening to a friend or authority. If we hear someone "reading" to us, we won't be drawn to what is being said. That can be a big waste of your advertising dollars.

166

AdSense not only involves the way we think about advertising and marketing, but it also involves the words we use to express our message and the way we express the words paralinguistically.

When you once get a person's full attention,
then is the time to accomplish all you ever hope
with them. Cover every phase of your subject.
One fact leads to some, one to another. Omit
any one and a certain percentage will lose the
fact which might convince. In one reading
of an advertisement, one decides for
or against a proposition.

~Claude Hopkins

Chapter Eighteen
The Message –
Writing Effective Traditional Copy

So how should you write effective copy for the micro-advertiser? It is, of course, a rhetorical question. There are so many factors to consider. But first I will address writing copy for traditional media, then for website content.

What kind of business do you have? That's imperative to know. You write copy differently for each type of business.

What is your competition doing? Are they aggressive or passive? Are there many of them, or just one or two? Do you want to dominate, or just compete? This is where positioning comes into play.

What is your location relative to your competitors? What are the advantages you have over your competitors? The disadvantages?

If there is a distinct, recognizable disadvantage, it should be addressed in the message.

Remember with consistency the public will believe your message... eventually. Take the Toyota dealer who ranked in about the middle of the pack in retail sales among 12 Toyota dealers in a major market. His ad campaign focused on one consistent element. The General Manager, who did his own spots, said in every ad "We're going to be #1 soon."

He developed a multi-media campaign including billboards, radio, and television. And in every single ad, he claimed his aspiration. He didn't say, "We want to be #1." He said, "We're going to be #1 soon."

Within a year he was well on his way. Only one problem, though. He kept the campaign going too long. After five years of saying, "We're going to be #1 real soon," the public caught on that they never were going to be #1. And he never was.

Now take my example earlier of the Dodge dealer who proclaimed himself to be "Atlanta's Dodge Giant." The smallest dealer lot in town became Atlanta's Dodge Giant within a year.

Did you notice in both examples that it took a year? Remember realistic expectations? A lot of businesses have written copy points such as these and kept it up for two or three months. They get frustrated because business hasn't turned around and they change direction. They lose a lot of money in residual effect. They either run out of patience, or they run out of money.

I handle the advertising for one of the nation's largest floor covering stores, Carpets of Dalton, in Dalton Georgia, the carpet capitol of the world. For over six years, they used Don Sutton, the great Atlanta Braves sports announcer and Hall of Fame pitcher, as their on-camera spokesperson.

About the time I took over the account, we quit using him. Several years later, I still heard, "Oh, that's the carpet store that Don Sutton talks about." The residual effect can be tremendous, but it takes a lot of time and money to build that residual.

Swaying the public takes time, money and patience. Especially if you have nothing better than rhetoric to distinguish yourself from your competitor. Even, as we said earlier, if the rhetoric is true.

Every commercial needs three elements: an attention getter, a salient point and a call to action. First, you must determine your desired result. Then define your salient point.

For example, if the desired result is for someone to pick up the telephone and call your number then the salient point would be your phone number.

Consider advertising you see for personal injury attorneys. A lot of people among the legal community look down on it as "schlock" advertising, but that's their elitist opinion.

It is a profession and a very competitive one. Just look online for the personal injury attorney near you. They're as plentiful as convenience stores.

Why is it considered demeaning to the legal profession to run an ad for a personal injury attorney on television during a daytime soap opera? You'd have to ask an attorney. Why do P.I. attorneys do it? It makes good marketing sense, and it is the most cost-effective way for them to advertise. Let's analyze the salient audience.

Who would call a P.I. attorney? Someone who has either been injured in a serious accident or knows someone who has. These are the only people who would potentially respond to this message on any given day.

A person injured in an accident who is sitting in front of television would call a P. I. attorney. That makes sense too. If they're seriously injured, they are somewhere recuperating, usually at home. The television is right there in the bedroom. That's why daytime television makes sense. It is one of the least expensive day-parts, and television has a captured audience.

The people who respond to P.I. advertising are primarily low-middle to middle-class citizens. That is television's primary audience.

Now that we've identified our salient audience and our result, it's easy to describe the salient message.

"If you've been injured in an accident call this number." Any attempt to stray away from this method will result in an increased opportunity for failure.

If you've ever watched daytime television in most markets, or if you go online, you will see an abundance of attorney ads. They all have the same underlying message. "If you've been injured in an accident call this number." So how do you get your message to stand out? You do it by "dressing up" the salient point. This is where the creativity comes in.

There are many talented, creative copywriters in the world. But you must be talented and creative after you have developed your salient point and determined your desired result. Otherwise, your ad might win awards but fail to get adequate results. It's like being all dressed up with no place to go.

What are some tips for "dressing up" your message so it will stand out? Here are some suggestions.

One way is to brand your business with a recognizable music bed. I don't mean a silly jingle that sounds like it was produced in the 1960s. You know the ones I'm talking about, the ones with the easy listening singers.

> We'll treat you special,
> We'll treat you like friends,
> From our service to our sales,
> We'll follow the trends.
> Get the best deal today
> From your friendly Ford dealer.
> Joe Smith Ford on Broadview at Peeler!

Yuck! No, don't waste your money on that. Your music doesn't even need words. Just a good, dynamic music bed that the public hears every time they listen to your ad.

Make sure the music compliments the delivery. If your message is urgent, use urgent music. If your message is placid, use appropriate music.

Find a recognizable, consistent voice. I can always tell when I hear a movie promo for a Disney film. You know the voice I'm talking about: that friendly, sincere, unthreatening voice introducing, "The exploits of seven unforgettable dwarfs and the beautiful Show White."

Avoid trying to tell the audience your entire story in 60 seconds or 30 seconds. Remember, the audience isn't there to listen to your ads. If you haven't caught their attention in the first 3 seconds you've lost their attention.

Don't try to reach everyone with one message. Department store newspaper ads are a good example. They will run a full page ad promoting a storewide one-day sale, but the ad will show a woman or two in casual dresses, promoting the junior miss department.

What about the men's department, or fragrances, or jewelry or housewares? A department store has something for everyone, but the ads focus on only one point. Believe me. The public gets the idea. They'll be drawn to the store by knowing it's a one-day event, and they'll pass all those other departments on the way to the junior miss department. They're checking things out in the aisles all the way.

Laundry listing, as it is known, is effective for tire stores and grocery sale days because people are perusing those ads for a specific purpose.

Don't try to tell your entire story. Just tell enough to get the public's interest. If you do that effectively, they'll take the effort to find out more.

I discourage my clients from putting street addresses in their radio ads. It is wasting valuable seconds and the people driving around in their cars cannot write down the address. Give them a recognizable landmark. They'll find you.

If you don't have an easily recognizable phone number, don't use it in radio or TV ads. People know how to find your number if you've gotten their interest. And in today's world, it is on your webpage.

Even in print ads, you shouldn't give away too much information. People have a tendency to fill every available inch of the ad for which they are paying a considerable price. It is the ad with a lot of white space that usually attracts your eyes.

The print ad should be visually appealing to your audience. Notice how quick and simple it is to divert your eyes from this page you are reading. Once the eyes are diverted in the newspaper, the prospect is lost. If every other ad is cluttered, and most of them are, just imagine how yours will stand out if it is not cluttered.

Over the years I have assigned students the task of writing a 60-second radio ad. The topics varied, the delivery varied, but over 90% of the time, one thing was constant. Most of them tried to fill the entire 60 seconds with words. That's a natural tendency. It's easy to write 60 seconds worth of copy and slap some music behind it. The challenge is to be creative: to go "outside the box."

Chick-Fil-A, the successful Atlanta-based fast food franchise, developed a great campaign: "outside the box." They utilized billboards, a one-dimensional medium with definite size parameters.

Their message was cute. They used cows painting the billboard with catch phrases like, "Eat More Chicken." And they always spelled a word or two wrong.

The trick, though, was to actually construct life-size cows, climbing ladders and holding paintbrushes, suggesting they had just painted the sign. That is being "outside the box!"

Don't try to fill your box with too much information. For instance, in radio ads use sound effects to separate or reinforce the words. Radio is called "the theater of the mind." The opportunity to create any scenario is as endless as your creativity.

By creating and publishing remarkable content in the form that educates, informs, inspires and entertains, marketers can begin to build relationships with prospects early on in the buying cycle.

~Jonathon Lister

Chapter Nineteen
The Message–Writing Effective
Digital Content

Having a great looking website is one thing. Being able to use it effectively in search engine optimization is another thing. Without good content it's like being all dressed up with no place to go. Having poor content will ultimately get you nowhere. It will only result in a waste of time, energy and resources.

It takes more than just creative writing. I have met literally hundreds of recent, young college graduates with good writing skills. They are very adept at the English language. These children of the digital age, young people who grew up with a computer within reach every day, will open digital marketing firms and charge you an arm and a leg to manage your digital marketing. They are creative in designing attractive websites and writing appealing content, but most of them fail miserably in their endeavors. Believe me, I have worked with dozens of companies who spent a lot of money on digital design and advertising and gotten nowhere.

There is a clear path for content marketers that can lead to boosting SEO rankings and bring qualified traffic to your website. By writing original content search engines can help your site gain exposure. Google, for instance, rewards high quality sites that contain original content. Good content will make a better website and improve your rankings. Bad content will fail just about every time.

The first principle of great content is using original content. Some digital companies hire exceptional writers who deliver original content every hour of every day. But it is not enough to be a good original writer. As is the case with traditional content writing, the skilled writer is someone who should understand behavioral science. They concentrate all their efforts on getting into the head of your prospective client. They don't write for themselves, their likes or dislikes, they write with the consumer in mind. What are their habits? What makes them decide which product or service they want to use? What makes them tick? Writers like this are few and far between. But it is essential in writing good content.

Rehashing the same concepts or following other posts over and over is not original. Remember, when hiring a good firm to help you improve your digital marketing you get what you pay for! A lot of business try to cut corners and pay as little as possible. Or they try to do it themselves with little, or no experience in content writing. Also make sure they follow this rule...if you don't have anything useful to say, don't say it.

Another rule for writing good content is to focus on very strong headlines. It is said that 80% of people will read your headlines, but only 20% will read the rest of your content. The headline is as important as the article or post itself.

In writing good internet ad copy you must create an enticing offer. The best ads ever written got nowhere if they didn't attract a prospective client with a reason to respond. When writing your copy, you need to know what keywords...words or phrases that someone would type in if they were looking for your product, advice or services...and use those keywords in the body of text. There are tools like Wordtracker which allows you to see what words people are using in their searches.

Don't try to sell everything you have to offer in one ad. The purpose of advertising is to get people to respond, not just be entertained. If you have a department store that sells hundreds of items, you don't want to put every item and every price, in one ad. The ad would be too cluttered and would not be read. Choose loss leaders, or items that no one else can offer, and focus on those. Once you get their attention they will pursue more information.

Try to make the content personable. Talk to the person you are trying to reach like they are your friend or neighbor, not a prospect. Decide who your audience is and talk their language. Don't assume they all understand what you're trying to say through your perspective. Understand their perspective. Hit the emotions.

And don't assume everyone will buy the moment they see your ad. Today's savvy generation of skeptics aren't as impulsive as their parents. They want to learn more, digest the information you've given them, compare options and make a careful deliberation before spending their money. The good content writer for websites leads the public into further research on the site they are visiting, and doesn't allow them to pursue other options. Don't try to "hard sell" like so much traditional advertising attempts. People are turned off by it after years of letdowns. Research and fully understand what the potential consumer thinks, believes and follows. Learn the language that they speak. Learn how they like to be addressed. And find subtle ways to encourage a call to action. These things are hard to do. Not everyone can write copy effectively. That's why so many advertising campaigns fail.

Make sure that your content gives the reader a sense of how to apply the information. Tell them how to use the material, don't just present the material. Assume that you are teaching them something they have never heard before, and write it in a way that they will appreciate your efforts. You must be able to provide answers to their potential questions. After all, the purpose of a search engine is to deliver a set of answers. How do I do this? Who do I call? What are my choices? These factors are extremely important when writing original content.

Make sure your content is accurate. Good content writers will do the research and find more than one backup source to the information they present. The first time the public sees anything that smacks of falsehood you will lose them forever. Make sure your content is accurate, thought provoking and engaging. Make sure your readers reflect on what they have read. People love stories, so use an anecdote that clarifies the point you want to make.

You can make your content more interesting by including creative images and videos. People have different ways of learning. Highly cerebral people like reading and digesting content. Other people are more influenced when you can show them a picture. Neither one of them is wrong, they just have different ways of picking up useful information.

And be certain to make continuous updates to your website or blog. Search engines don't favor sites that aren't updated on a regular basis. Do not create a blog post or any other content lightly. It is a difficult talent, and the good ones take time to research and write. Use proper grammar. And reread your content before you publish it. Are there words you can take out? Have you given the reader the best information you can?

If you own a business and want to develop, or fine tune, a company website you might want to think about hiring an experienced copywriter. I know, no one understands your business like you do. But that might be a problem more than a benefit. You might need someone outside your organization to offer perspective. They might see your business the way outsiders see your business, not the way you perceive your business to be.

Don't just dive in and try to sell your products or services Direct the copy points to your visitors. They don't really care about your company's philosophies. They are visiting your website because they have a question, a need or want a problem solved. Talk to them first, address their problems and needs. Then you can talk about you.

Understand that you are directing your writing to people, but you must also direct your writing for search engines. Getting search engines to deliver customers requires using the keywords they are using to search for you. Those keywords and phrases need to be in your content in order to be effective.

Don't use the typical advertising rhetoric. People are turned off to it because, as mentioned earlier in this book, they have been burned before. Give solid examples that help your visitor realize the excellence of your service or products. As copywriter Jonathan Kranz wrote, "If you want to scare the cloak off Little Red Riding Hood, don't lecture her about the woods and its perils. Put the wolf's hot breath on her neck!"

And finally create a good call to action, one that is believable. Whether it's an incredible offer, a request to subscribe to a newsletter, or a chance to engage in interactive discussion, if you don't give them something to respond to they will not continue the relationship you are attempting to create.

Ever heard the expression "all dressed up with no place to go"? You can hire internet companies that design aesthetically beautiful looking sites. But without the right content you will not get the results you want by developing the website in the first place. Dig deep to find creative designers, but place as much emphasis on hiring copywriters who understand what makes people respond to your uniqueness, and who know how to utilize that understanding in writing copy that works.

Advertisement is the lubricant for the free enterprise system.

~Lee Arthur Keimenson

Chapter Twenty
The Evolution of Advertising

The future of advertising for the micro-advertiser looks dim. Sources of media, both traditional and digital, increase almost proportionately to the rise in media costs. As the global village grows, our avenues to information and entertainment become more abundant. Unfortunately, our population isn't growing at nearly the same rate as this avalanche of information.

In the middle of all this growth began the computer age. It snuck up on the baby boom generation, with one of its own changing the world. Bill Gates brought the world into everyone's home with his Microsoft. Suddenly, almost overnight, every corner of the world...sources of knowledge, sources of information, sources of people and places...were at our fingertips, in a way that was faster and more abundant than we've ever known in our history.

The small businesses that must survive in this over-communicated society are engulfed by more competition, rising media costs, and by the dilemma of how to reach their audience most effectively and efficiently.

Why are media costs rising so much? The cost of a television ad in the 6 o'clock news in most markets has increased by nearly 400% in recent decades. Radio ad costs have grown at the same rate Rising newspaper rates increased about 200% during the same period, while the circulation has decreased. That was the death of the industry. Digital costs increase as well as the places you can spend your digital dollars.

During this time frame the people who work in the media business are earning much more than they were a decade earlier. Today mega-corporations are acquiring every radio and television station they can gobble up, which means higher corporate expenses, thus the need to charge higher rates to cover them. This phenomenon really began in the 1970s. The entrepreneurs of media foresaw a way to make small fortunes by selling these stations to the highest bidders. When the stations were purchased the new owners would put them back on the auction block and nearly double or triple their profits within a few years.

This turnover continued at a torrid pace until about 1990, when the huge corporations and public companies were ready to pounce with the really big money. Imagine the debt service! Today, the cost of maintaining these operations is very forbidding. And advertising is still the only source of revenue. It is little wonder that media rates have increased so much. And in the recent past these same mega-companies realized the profit in digital so they started focusing on these products too.

As newspaper circulations declined dramatically in just about every market in the country local television newscasts also showed a dissatisfaction among viewers. According to a national survey by Insite Media Research 22 percent of adults completely avoid local TV news, about double from the number 10 years ago.

And now...the Internet! A computer in every American home, and a cell phone within reach of all of them, the formerly exclusive sources of advertising information had to give way for the big elephant in the room. Advertisers are now taking their message to cyberspace in hopes of capturing audiences.

What impact will this have on the potential results traditional advertising? The businesses that must advertise to capture their share of the marketplace will have to be more innovative and aggressive.

How aggressive should the survivors be? I recently heard a story about a college football game ending on a bad call. A defender went for an interception in the end zone and it was ruled a turnover. Television instant replay clearly showed that the ball hit the ground first, but the defender put on an award winning show and the evidence wasn't clear enough for the referees to overturn the call. The player knew the ball hit the ground, but the referee didn't see it. Unfortunately for the opposing team it was the game-ending play. The host of a radio talk show where I heard the story posed the question of whether there was a boundary between gamesmanship and ethics. It is an interesting question in the field of marketing and advertising.

At what point in the heat of battle does fairness have to set in? I surmise that professional sports are played as a war. What is fair in war? Did the dropping of the atomic bomb on Hiroshima to end World War II go beyond the bounds of fairness?

Business is like war too. If 65% of all businesses fail within 5 years what can an entrepreneur do to fight off the competition, survive and grow...within legal bounds? Should businesses put on kid's gloves for fear of overstepping the rules of competition?

The survival of the fittest *should* be the rule in the business world. If you do not go into business with the attitude and the commitment to be successful at the expense of smaller competitors, you should expect to follow a rugged road.

The computer age has changed the landscape of the playing field for the participants in the survival of the fittest. The lower and middle classes and the minorities who are now placed lower in the caste system will be better able to compete in the global marketplace. No one can see them. They can only see their intellect, which is determined by the way they communicate on a keyboard.

In the past advertising directed potential customers to make a phone call or drive to a location to get the merchandise they wanted. Now advertising directs consumers to a web page. And just as is the case in traditional advertising the webpage will have to convince a skeptic.

We are skeptics because we are assaulted by the rhetoric of advertising and are constantly disappointed by the product or service we are lured to. We feel duped by the words, whether spoken or written, and are more cautious the next time we hear them.

As I mentioned earlier, once you have determined the actual response you want to elicit from your ad you have a limited space or time frame in which to accomplish your goal. A radio or television spot has to convince us to respond in 30 or 60 seconds. Now, all you have to do with your advertising is simply direct someone to a web page. It doesn't take that much time or space to do this effectively.

Today's advertising geniuses are the designers of the web pages…the ones who tease you, through the simplicity of words, pictures and phrases, to get you to go beyond the home page and explore. You can sell your image, the advantages of your product or service, and even guide your audience into contacting you for more information by clicking a call button on the webpage and being directly connected to the company you are seeking. That is something that was impossible to accomplish in 30 or 60 seconds. And this is a perfect way to build a client base.

What you do with your database can save you a lot of money on advertising, and keep you in touch with your target market on a personal basis. Of course, with the database you need your own website. With a database you can learn your customer's preferences, when they buy and what they buy.

With a database of customers, you have an accurate picture of the number of people who receive your message, you can count how many people respond to your message and you can measure the conversion rates of people who try free demos, order a sample, subscribe to your newsletter, emails blasts or newsletters to buy your product.

When you have a good website up and running you will need to manage it diligently to get the most effectiveness from it. You must promote it and get your potential customers to provide the necessary information so you can stay informed about them, their lifestyles and habits. You can customize the experience of your on-line presentation to specific psychographics.

Once this is done you can save on printing and postage while keeping your clients informed. The necessity, and the huge expense of these major advertising revenue sources, have been eliminated by a simple click.

The other entrepreneurs of advertising are the ones who know how to get potential consumers to your web page...the keyboard kids with the corporate connections.

Buying products and services has become commonplace on the Internet as e-commerce, a term never before used in the history of economic expansion prior to the 2000s, becomes the king- maker.

But how do we determine which product or service we should choose as we swim through a myriad of choices in the waves of the web? The information we receive will continue to be important in our choices, but the basic nature of advertising will remain...image *is* everything! And the images are still created by traditional mass media.

Will the nature of shopping change, leaving us with a vast wasteland of mall cemeteries on deserted lots, and strip centers decaying in the suburbs? You can now do all your grocery shopping without leaving your home. Will this be the end of supermarkets as we know them?

The answer is probably no. It is a basic human need to interact on a social level. The malls and movie theaters and grocery stores are still the town squares of our society.

As I said, to get people to your website you still need mass media. You might have the best web site in the world, but if no one knows about it, it's like being all dressed up with no place to go. People must find you, and they must want to come back to your home page, just like you need to give them a pleasant experience when they come to your location. If not, they won't come back. That has not changed, and will never change. Get people to your web site through your advertising image, and let the information on the page reinforce the image.

E-commerce has definitely had an effect on retail shopping. To what extent it continues to erode is hard to say. It depends on the nature of the business. In the waterbed wars of the 1980s many young entrepreneurs became wealthy through the benefits of sleeping on water. But in the late 1980s the war ended and only the strong survived. That is because only about 20% of us desire to sleep on a flotation device... period! The other 80% want to keep sleeping the way they have always slept. So when the waterbed market reached its critical mass, no amount of advertising could change the *creature of habit*.

There will be a critical mass of e-buyers too. I believe automobile purchases will eventually account for less than half of the retail business that car dealers get, but probably won't go beyond that point. Humans still want to smell the new car showroom, negotiate with the salespeople and kick the tires. They will still desire to walk the lot and make a choice. And that will continue for as long as free enterprise allows negotiability.

For products or services that are less negotiable, the Internet will capture a larger share of the business. Music stores and book stores, for instance, have suffered because it became cheaper to purchase music on line. And you don't have to wait a few days for your product to get to your mailbox.

For the small businesses AdSense will be essential in order to survive. If we are bombarded with up to 5,000 messages a day now it could increase to nearly 10,000 messages with the addition of new mediums and increased opportunities. The micro-advertisers will diminish with time as large, powerful public companies devour the marketplace and the minds of the consumer.

Here is some advice. For the remainder to survive you must determine the *purpose* of your advertising. Decide on the end result, the behavioral response you want to elicit through your advertising dollars. Don't waste your money on messages that don't have a call to action.

Learn to *position* your product. Learn and understand the marketing plan of your competitors. Base your journey toward success on realistic expectations.

Understand what it will take to achieve success, and hold on to that success If you solicit expertise and advice, choose your counselors wisely. Don't just look at their awards. Look at their ability to get you *results*.

Get your head out of your ads if you don't understand AdSense. More than one aspiring entrepreneur has failed when they let their ego control their destiny.

Understand the strengths and weaknesses of all the media available to you. Use AdSense in determining your media buy. Don't allow the media to use your advertising dollars to fill holes. Remember, if an ad falls in the forest and there is no one around to hear it will it make a noise?

Learn how to add salience to your marketing. Identify your salient audience and your salient point. If the message is aimed at the needs, dreams and desires of your audience your chance for success increases.

Avoid the rhetoric that has engulfed our advertising vocabulary. Understand that the public has become immune to it. The messages have become redundant, rhetorical and resilient. This is a combination that will lead to failure.

All this is easier said than done. But learn to think and plan as a behavioral scientist and you will be a step ahead of the other survivors.

The nature of advertising is indeed changing every single day because the nature of commerce is changing. And it is changing in whirlwind proportions.

Who could have predicted in 1950 that the average home would have nearly 150 choices in television stations by 2000? Who could have predicted in 1950 that the average American would have access to every corner of the world by 1980? And all at the click of a button in the comfort of their home. Who would have predicted in 1950 that you could make a phone call from anywhere within the boundaries of a cell tower, or click a button to get directions, or immediately text a friend or family member that you will be there shortly?

And who can predict the possibilities in the year 2050? Will malls and movie theaters, grocery stores and car lots, be extinct? Where will the work force migrate? And what will happen to our social skills as we decrease our social exposure

One of the hazards of the digital revolution's rapid advance on the world of advertising and marketing is that the generation gap is very small, but huge in impact. The children of the digital age disregard traditional advertising, calling it a dinosaur. They believe major media like television is dying quickly. But will traditional media go away? Not likely! Consider the billions of dollars that is derived each year through advertising. It will not all go to digital advertising, because in many cases digital advertising on its own will not be effective because of the global competition. People's media habits might change with the growth of Hulu and Netflix and other methods of viewing entertainment that are introduced continuously. But people will still wake up and turn on the television or radio to see what happened while they were sleeping, and turn it on at night, if for nothing else than create "white noise" by which people fall asleep. New ways of getting advertising messages to the public through traditional branding, or outbound advertising, will never go away. It will be reinvented and infused into our daily habits.

And so many traditional advertising experts waited too late to catch up with the digital world. Many of them believe the digital age is just a passing fad and everything will come back to traditional messaging. But everyone should realize that the blend of traditional media and digital media will continue to create a dynamic that will help businesses market their wares to the public. Dogmatic views of the global village will not help economies grow and businesses compete. Traditional media and digital media both need to realize that one does not supersede each other.

If done properly they can only enhance each other.

As witnessed by the digital revolution, technology changes, culture and the ways we engage with each other change over time, but human behavior doesn't change....it just adapts. The future is in the hands of the cyber generation. These entrepreneurs must allow us to progress cautiously and deliberately to our destiny. The consequences of their failure could cause a lot of turmoil, as well as heartache, in our society. Social and economic collapse could be the result. AdSense will allow us to survive as a business community. Common sense will allow us to survive as a society.

www.ingramcontent.com/pod-product-compliance
Lightning Source LLC
Chambersburg PA
CBHW032006170526
45157CB00002B/565